Death by Screens: How to Present Digital-Design Work and L

By Ben Sauer

ISBN: 978-1-7393557-0-8

For my parents

Patricia and Gerard Sauer

"We need to find out: Do they make conscious choices? Or is their motivation so instinctive that they don't understand a 'why' question at all?

And... and biggest of all, we need to have enough vocabulary with them that we understand their answer."

Dr Louise Banks, *Arrival* (2016)

Contents

CHAPTER 5

Writing: sharpen your rationale with well-crafted words 67

CHAPTER 6

Slides: design for listening, not reading 79

Death by Screens

Imagine someone gave you six months to create your dream design for a product. With all that time, you can think deeply about the problem, research, iterate, craft, and test every element. By the end, you've created the thing you're most proud of. Then you are given thirty minutes to meet with the CEO, who will decide whether to invest in launching the product. This one meeting will determine whether the world will ever see your design.

As you prepare to present, you're faced with an unfortunate paradox: the quality of the design work you show in this meeting is less important than your ability to explain and sell it. You can be an exceptional designer with world-changing ideas, but if you can't present well, none of that really matters. Great design is not always *obviously* great. To sell your work, you need to answer the most important question.

"Why is it like that?"

In the 2009 documentary *Objectified*, Jony Ive summed up the way a designer looks at the world: "You're constantly looking at something and thinking, 'Why is it like *that* and not like *this*?'"

I remember the first time I encountered tactile paving in the UK. Walking towards a road crossing, I felt a pattern of small dome-shaped bumps beneath my feet. After a few more encounters, I wondered: why were some bumps arranged in a grid and others in a diagonal pattern? For whom was the design intended? A few weeks later, I learned that the patterns of the bumps signalled different hazards for the visually impaired. A square grid meant "cross the road here", and a diagonal pattern meant "edge of train platform". Whenever I can't understand why a design is the way it is, I think back to this moment.

Sometimes that moment of confusion results from bad design, but often, it happens because we simply don't know the context of use. What scenario was the designer thinking about? Who is the user? What journey are they on? The people to whom designers present will often lack that same context. They don't understand *why* we designed something in a particular way. We open our favourite design tools, show them our carefully designed screens, and expect them to *just get it*. But they don't. Performers die on stage when they commit the cardinal sin of boring their audience, and the same is true for designers. When we present screen after screen of design work without engaging people, their eyes glaze over, and they lose interest. It's death by screens, for them and us. Fortunately, there's a way to avoid this unfortunate fate. If you want your stakeholders to understand not just *what* you designed, but *why*, tell them a story.

This book is about the story we must craft around our designs. It's about explaining how we intend our designs to be used, not simply how we intend them to appear. When we leave out the story of use, we leave a gap in understanding. And in that gap, strange things grow in the minds of our audience: boredom, speculation, doubt, mistrust, unhelpful suggestions, and off-topic questions. A good story closes that gap, engages our audience's interest, puts our work into context, and facilitates a better understanding of the work than the screens could ever do on their own. As designer and author Mike Monteiro says, "Design can't speak for itself".[1]

Our true canvas is not the screen. It is behaviour: what screens enable people to do. We must focus on telling *that* story. And what is a story, at its most basic level, if not the story of some human behaviour? When we try to explain a series of screens by talking through what's on them, it's like reading a comic strip with no dialogue. It's so much easier to explain why a design is the way it is with a story about what happens when someone uses it. And as you practise telling stories about your design, you will find that the hard work of explaining the design rationale melts away.

As human beings, we are wired to transmit and receive information through stories. It's how people have passed information from generation to generation for thousands of years. In the age of data and short-form content, it's easy to forget just how receptive people will be to a good story. Not only that, but good storytelling also means you probably won't need to show them all the work. Good stories result from judicious editing. Tell a good story, and your audience will trust you with everything else.

This book: how it can help you

If you're a digital product designer struggling to present your work, this book is for you. I wrote it because I'm a public speaker and designer; I learned how to combine these skills through years of giving talks at conferences worldwide and presenting my design work in high-stakes scenarios. To research how I could help you, I interviewed designers about what they struggled with, and the following problems became the focus of this book.

You need help with what and how to present

You have no problem designing great-looking presentations, but you struggle to know *what* to present and *what not* to. How much detail should you go into? What should you present, aside from the design? What should you say, and in what order? You've also struggled with *how* to present. You're not a public speaker, and so you lack confidence when standing up in front of an audience. This book will help you figure out the less obvious parts of creating a great presentation.

You've struggled to articulate your design choices

Much of your day-to-day work is intuitive. When you're in the process of designing something, you're not forced to articulate why you make the choices you do. Therefore, it can be hard to explain these choices to others or remember why things are the way they are. This book will teach you how to articulate and defend your design choices.

Presenting is an emotional challenge

More than with most meetings you attend, you feel anxious before presenting your work; it feels like a reflection of how valuable you are as a person. You haven't had a lot of chances to practise presenting (it isn't even taught in some design courses). You lack the confidence to have productive conversations with stakeholders. Maybe you've even 'died' a few times already, figuratively speaking. This book will give you a framework for discussing the design with your stakeholders.

To tackle these problems, this book will show you how to deliver an agency-style presentation: a high-stakes, high-effort presentation for a less-familiar audience. Even if you don't present often, practising for a high-stakes presentation will give you many skills you can apply elsewhere. The day-to-day work of an in-house product designer doesn't offer many opportunities to practise high-effort communication. But learning works best when you are challenged beyond your current abilities, and it's the best way to gain influence.

In this book, we'll use the fictional example of an in-house designer presenting to the leadership of a food delivery start-up. It's a high-stakes presentation because a radical change is being proposed to the interface, and because the designer hasn't presented to the leadership team before.

NOTE » High-stakes presentations aren't always the best method of communicating with stakeholders. Relying on them can create communication debt. For more on this, see the Useful Extras section at the back of the book.

HIGH ON STAKES, LOW ON CLOTHING

When I was at university, my friend Matt wrote a Pinteresque play and asked me to audition for a part. Even though I wasn't very interested in acting, I tried out and got the role. Unfortunately, I failed to read the whole script until later, which was a big mistake. In a scene I'd skipped, my character lost a strip-poker game and had to appear nude on stage. Despite all my instincts telling me to quit, I went through with it.

In hindsight, being nude on stage was one of the most useful experiences of my life. I still get nervous before any performance, but once you've done something like that, nothing else seems quite so scary anymore. There are many, much less scary paths to being a confident performer. I tell this story only to illustrate the following point: high-stakes situations are the best opportunity for personal growth. And if you're not in one, practise like you are. You learn the most when you challenge yourself.

If you're short on time...

- **Scan the table of contents.** It will provide a digest of many lessons I share in this book.

- **Follow the suggested presentation structure.** If you only have a few days, or even hours, to prepare a design presentation, use the structure suggested in chapters three and four to put something together quickly.

- **Use the preparation checklist.** Throughout the book, I provide tasks to complete. They're collated for quick reference in 'Useful Extras' at the end of the book.

If you have more time, follow the chapters in order as you prepare your presentation. The time you invest will pay off later. This book doesn't labour any topics and mostly skips the theory; you will see examples and you can apply what you learn quickly.

Why stories work: people are hard-wired to pay attention to them

Humans have told stories to teach and communicate since ancient times. We won't cover much theory about how stories work, but it helps to know some key points about what makes a good one.

1. Stories focus on a character and their challenge

If we want to get our stakeholders out of their heads and empathising with our users, there's no better method than a good story. Engaging stories have someone to root for—a hero—and something they're fighting against, like a challenge or a villain. To paraphrase designer and programmer Kathy Sierra, this is why we create products. Good ones make people better versions of themselves; they become heroes in their own life stories. "Don't make a better [x]," she says, "make a better [user of x]".[2]

2. Good stories stay on track

Good stories avoid too many rabbit holes and distractions. Imagine a more realistic version of *The Simpsons* in which we see Homer working in real-time at the power plant. We'd see him spending hours slaving away pushing buttons, but we'd be bored as hell watching it. Edit out the distracting, irrelevant parts of your presentation as ruthlessly as you do with your designs. There are many more things you *could* include than what you *should*. The danger for us designers is that we've spent so much effort on our designs we think we *have* to explain it all.

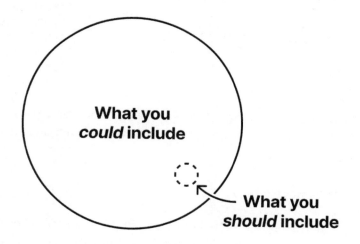

3. Story structures have patterns and shapes

Have you noticed that in the last few decades, Hollywood movies tend to start with a big-bang opening sequence? Writers have learned the story shapes that hold our attention and use this knowledge to craft the ups and downs of their films. Creating a presentation without crafting the structure is like designing a website without considering the information architecture. Far too many design presentations follow the most obvious order: the design process. The problem is that stakeholders don't really need to know much about it.

Here's a commonly used story structure, 'Man in Hole', as identified by Kurt Vonnegut.[3] The protagonist begins in a place where life is mostly fine.

Then, disaster strikes, and they must battle through adversity towards a happy ending.

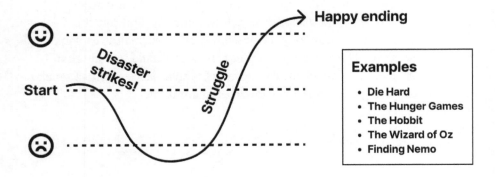

You don't need to be a Vonnegut-level storyteller to deliver a great presentation, but you do need to consider how to hold your audience's attention.

4. Good stories flow

Figuring out your story structure before creating any content allows your story to flow. Each section should follow the last one with good reason. That doesn't mean a chronological story is always the right approach. Rather, it means you have considered how the order of each 'scene' will affect your audience's understanding of your design.

Matt Stone and Trey Parker, the creators of *South Park*, follow a simple rule: bad stories use '*and then*' between each scene, they are just a sequence of events. Good stories use '*and therefore*', '*so*', '*but*', or '*however*': events build on one another to form a cohesive whole. How they're connected matters. Compare these two examples from the life story of coach and speaker Jeff Gothelf:[4]

> **Bad story:** I graduated and then I joined the circus and then I met the human cannonball and then he told me how he got his job.

Good story: I graduated with no plan so I joined the circus therefore I met some crazy characters like the human cannonball, but his story was nothing like I imagined.

You'll use this method later to evaluate the strength of your story's glue, the space between the screens that holds it all together.

CHAPTER 2

First steps: prepare early to save time later

A manager at Greenpeace once shared the following mnemonic with their team: "Perfect Preparation Prevents Piss Poor Performance". This is true, but our need to prepare isn't just a performance issue, it's the thing that is most likely to build confidence. When you are mindful of what and how to prepare, and give yourself more time than you think you'll need, you will reduce your anxiety about the whole process.

Know your stakeholders: map your audience's concerns and expertise

Many designers, when faced with challenges in their organisations, fall into 'us vs. them' thinking. A team of designers likes to complain about 'the business' and claim that "they just don't understand design!" This may be true, but it's also incomplete. If 'they' don't understand design, it's your job to help them understand. You don't really need them to understand design as a discipline, but you do need them to understand your design rationale, the reasons you made the choices you did.

It's also not productive to think of these people as separate from you. Stakeholders are your collaborators. Even when they don't 'get' your work, they are experts in their domain. By default, you should value their input. If a comedian bombs with a joke that people don't get, they don't sit there and blame the audience; they iterate. Even superstars like Chris Rock or Sarah Silverman start the process of creating a new comedy show in small clubs, revising the new material for a year or more until it works for a huge crowd.

Maybe you've never received useful feedback on your designs from stakeholders before. If that's true, it might be worth trying harder to find some. Not only are you seeking to help them understand your design, but you also want to turn them into excellent collaborators along the way. Great collaborators know how to give good feedback and add value by sharing their expertise. When stakeholders understand the rationale of designers, they turn from judges into collaborators.

Empathise with your stakeholders. Think ahead about how they can contribute usefully. This can be as quick and simple as creating a table like the one that follows. Use it to map out who each person is, what motivates them, and how their expertise can add value to the discussion.

Who	Role	Expertise	Challenge	Approach
Michela	CEO	Vision & strategy	Poker face in groups	1:1 feedback beforehand
Monique	Head of Engineering	Feasibility	Play devil's advocate	Have alternatives ready
Drew	Chief Product Officer	Roadmap	Numbers numbers numbers	Include potential growth numbers
Azeem	Head of Marketing	Brand	Nitpicks	Request content feedback in 1:1 session

When you know this, you can tailor your presentation to the audience as needed. Note the 'challenge' and 'approach' columns. If what you're presenting will be unexpected, or if a particular person is known for providing challenging feedback, you need to consider that now. For example, you may not have included any talking points about how your design speaks to the brand's values, but if you know you're presenting to the head of marketing, you now know a question about it might come up. You can avoid many unhelpful feedback discussions or concerns if you anticipate them in your planning.

It's also important to consider who is not invited and whether they should be. This group may include people who might provide useful insight or information (like engineers) or others who haven't been invited as they're not considered part of the decision-making team.

TASK » Use the table above to map out your attending stakeholders, their concerns, and your strategy.

TIP » If you're not familiar with the culture of the organisation you're presenting to, or if you have struggled to understand how it operates, read the section on culture fit in Useful Extras at the end of this book before getting started. It will help you adapt your presentation to suit the culture.

Choose your setting: take control of where, when, and how you present

Setting can determine success. Sometimes you will have control over where, when, and how you present. Other times you won't. But even the most junior designer can exert much more control than they realise. It takes some persistence but doing so will set you up for presentation success. The earlier you are in the process, the more time you have to exert control. Find a suitable setting and make sure the people you need to attend are free when you want, well in advance.

SEATING FOR SLEEPING

I once ran a workshop that began with a forty-five-minute talk introducing the subject matter. It was right after lunch, and I didn't know beforehand that the room only had beanbag chairs to sit on. Digesting their food, stretching out into a reclining posture, people felt a little too comfortable on those beanbags. Despite my best efforts with a tried-and-tested, engaging talk, a few people fell asleep before the activities. Small, overlooked details like this can kill your presentation; that's why planning ahead can make such a difference.

How to present: in-person or remote?

When planning a high-stakes design presentation, it's worth trying to have it in person if possible. In-person interactions will almost always guarantee more attention from your audience, are less socially awkward, and you can read the room. It's easier to have side chats or short one-to-one conversations before or after the meeting, which you can use to clarify understanding or address concerns. If you can't arrange an in-person meeting, don't worry, I'll provide tips for remote presentations later.

Where and when to present

Architecture and interior design can change how we feel within different spaces. Consider this when you choose where to present. The setting can affect how people receive your work in myriad, yet subtle, ways. The key factors to consider around the setting for your presentation are:

Room size and shape: Is the room so small that people will be crowded or so large it will be difficult for certain people to see the screen?

Light: Does the room have windows and natural light? Rooms with a view help us feel happier and more open-minded, while a windowless basement room can feel oppressive. On the flip side, will the sunlight inhibit a clear view of the screen? Are there blinds if you need them? How strong will the light be at the time of day you present?

Air and temperature: People have a hard time concentrating when it's too warm or they lack fresh air. Rooms with poor ventilation get worse throughout the day. If you present in the morning, the CO_2 level might be fine, but it might increase as the afternoon wears on, which can cause certain people to get headaches.

Time of day: A study by Jonathan Levav at Columbia University revealed that judges issued harsher sentences to guilty defendants right before lunch, presumably when they were feeling hungry.[5] Discourage unnecessarily tough criticism by providing snacks or choose a time when people aren't likely to be hungry. Mid-to-late afternoon is another slot to avoid, as people are generally tired and lose their ability to focus for longer periods of time. Ideally, present early to mid-morning when people are energised, or immediately after lunch when they're fed and happy but haven't hit the afternoon slump just yet.

TASK » Find and book a suitable time and space (or virtual space).

Send the invitation: attract constructive input by managing expectations

> You can lose even before you've entered the room.
> —Alastair Somerville

Most meeting invitations suck. They have an ill-thought-out, generic title, like 'June catchup' and include no agenda, so people don't know what will be going on or the purpose of the meeting. If we want collaborative discussion about our design, we should manage expectations beforehand.

In the invitation, remove any fuzziness about the purpose of the meeting and the work. You'll cover these again in the presentation for clarity (see the next chapter for more detail), but briefly, your email should cover:

1. **Why this meeting?** Explain whether you want alignment, input, or approval.

2. **Where are you in the process?** Briefly cover why you're meeting now

3. **Why this project?** Remind them what outcomes this work is supposed to deliver

Agenda overview
You don't need to cover the agenda in detail or include timings, but you do need to share the basics of what you'll cover.

Collaboration guidance
We want stakeholders to be in the right frame of mind to collaborate. We *don't* want them to come in thinking they will just sit there and judge your work, which is the common expectation. In chapter nine, we'll cover how to solicit good design feedback and how to keep the conversation inclusive. For now, just know that you can—and should—set expectations for this in advance.

Example invitation

SUBJECT: 'Menu for me' project: June design update

Hi everyone!

Here's a meeting invitation to update you on the latest design work for this project. We'd like to make sure we're all aligned about how we're proposing to change the app design.

The objective we will focus on is how we can encourage customers to try new food, based on what we've learned about them.

We've been designing and testing extensively, so we'd like to check in with you before committing any more time to production. If we've got this right, we can help users find new food to try, which will increase our conversion rate and retention.

In this meeting, we will:

- Tell you what we've learned
- Show the design
- Gather your feedback and questions

As useful feedback can come from anyone, we'll use a discussion format that will give everyone a chance to contribute.

We're excited to show you what we've got! See you there.

This invitation ensures that stakeholders are all on the same page before they enter and that they understand in advance this will be an inclusive discussion.

TASK » Send an invitation that manages expectations about the presentation.

Start with structure: work on the slides later

As designers, we're tempted to start preparing for a presentation by focusing on two things: the design process and showing the design work on the slides. You're *not* going to do this. To create a good story, outline the *structure* of the presentation first.

Outline horizontally

Use the next two chapters as a template for your outline. How you outline is of subtle importance. Most people outline in bullets, using a document or an outline tool, which gives you a vertical orientation. Instead, outline horizontally using sticky notes or a virtual whiteboard, as below. This format will allow you to see the shape of your story, where the highlights are, and where you might get bogged down in details. If you notice places where your audience's attention might slump, you can revise your presentation to address this before getting too far.

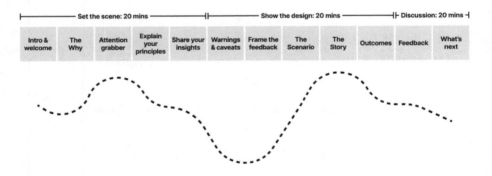

Outline the presentation structure horizontally so that you can see the ups and downs of your audience's attention.

NOTE » It's no accident that this method is similar to creating an experience map. To effectively communicate and persuade, we must craft the experience for stakeholders just like we would for users.

In this template outline, we have three sections of twenty minutes each: setting the scene, showing the design, and discussion afterwards. Most design presentations to stakeholders should be around the same length, between sixty and ninety minutes. If they're longer than that, you might be trying to show too much detail. What you say in between sections of your presentation will determine how well it flows.

CHAPTER 3

Structure part I: set the scene

In this chapter, you'll outline the first part of your presentation on sticky notes using the suggested sections below. These sections set the scene for the story you will tell about how the design will be used. Although you'll see example slides to explain each section in these two chapters, don't create any content of your own until after you're happy with your outline. By outlining first, you won't waste valuable time making content that may get cut later.

NOTE » The examples in the following chapters for this project are aspirational. You may not have as much certainty or evidence in your project, and that's okay. These examples demonstrate what you should aim for when you want to be clear and persuasive but aren't intended as a perfect fit for every situation: simplify and modify as needed.

Introductions and welcome: set yourself up as the host

Whether you're presenting in-person or remotely, you want your presentation to feel different to other meetings. Think of it like an occasion: you're having a great party, inviting people to participate in something special.

All good parties need a good host: this is the job you're performing when people arrive. This section is not so much about the content of your presentation but about the role you're performing as people enter. You want to achieve two results during this time:

1. Establish yourself as the host and facilitator, the person who will guide everyone. This is your meeting.

2. Create an informal, positive atmosphere that makes for better conversation later.

Here are tips on how to make this happen.

1. The greetings

Pay attention as people arrive. Smile, greet everyone, and introduce them to one another as needed. Engage in some light chat and make sure everyone is physically and socially comfortable.

For familiar, smaller audiences, ask questions about topics everyone is comfortable with to engage in conversation, e.g. "How did the launch party go, Sheena?" For larger, less-familiar audiences, ask questions that are broader, more inclusive, and require little effort to respond to, e.g. "How was everyone's long weekend?" You can make this even easier for remote audiences (where conversation is more difficult) by instructing them to post an emoji in the group chat.

2. Share a bit of yourself

In most cases, it's a good idea to share a little bit of yourself in this discussion. If you're going to ask them about their weekend, how was *yours*? Your behaviour sets the tone of the meeting. To get them sharing and talking informally, you need to set an example.

3. The micro-icebreaker

One easy way to get people talking informally is to show a question on the screen and invite them to discuss their answers with each other.

For example, let's say you want stakeholders to empathise with the user's challenge of choosing food. You can put a question on screen like the following one: you can break the ice and get everyone thinking about the challenge for users.

> **SAY »** "While you're getting settled, would anyone like to share their answer to this question?"

While people are coming in and getting settled, you can welcome them, do introductions, and get a discussion going about their answers.

TASK » Add 'Introductions and Welcome' to your outline.

Once everyone is settled, it's time to kick off the presentation.

The Whys: why this work, why now, and why this meeting

You've already touched on this in your invitation email, but you need to remind people of the important reasons you invited them to this meeting.

Why this work

Have you ever noticed a project drift? Where, by the time it was all done and dusted, people had forgotten what the original brief was? This happens during meetings, too. Your audience's minds will imagine all sorts of off-topic things while they're listening to you. To keep things on track, you must lay out that shared purpose as the principal topic of conversation. Be a beacon of clarity. The "why are we doing this?" in digital design work can vary, but let's stick to the most important reasons: solving a problem for users and meeting business objectives. Let's remind everyone why this work exists.

> **SAY »** "Okay, now that everyone is settled in, I'd like to get started. Thanks for making time to be here today. I'm excited to show you the work. I'd like to begin with a reminder of why we're working on this. Our objective is that we're..."

Our objective

User problem	**We're trying to help users find food they'd like to order...**
Business objective	**So that we can increase our conversion rate and retain our users**

> **SAY »** "Our hypothesis is that our new design, which learns about users' food preferences, will have these desired outcomes."

There. We've summarised the whole purpose of the work, included an element of reasonable doubt (the design is a hypothesis), and narrowed the scope of discussion. Later you should repeat your 'why' to keep the discussion on-track. Now that you've stated these objectives, you can follow with an evocative vision of the experience you're trying to create for users. Establishing a vision is useful for uniting your colleagues around a common cause: clarity has a compound effect.

SAY » "If we get this right, our ambition is to be the number one food-delivery app for people with dietary requirements, like vegans or those with allergies. They're not well served in today's market."

Our ambition

Be the go-to app for people with dietary requirements.

Status reminder: where are you in the process?

Stakeholders are busy people. While your project is the main preoccupation of your working life, it's one of fifty things in theirs. You can't expect them to remember all the details throughout the process; they need a reminder of the timeline. You're going to do this *briefly*. It's not good to use much detail about process anywhere in this presentation, as it's usually not interesting or useful. But you need to re-orient them to the work. Perhaps the last update was a month or two ago; they might need a brief reminder. Show them how the phases of work are connected:

a. where you've been

b. where you are now

c. what's next

You don't need to provide a lot of detail here, nor should you be super-accurate with timelines and dates. You just need to provide a rough concept about the sequence of events, enough to orient them to why you are meeting today.

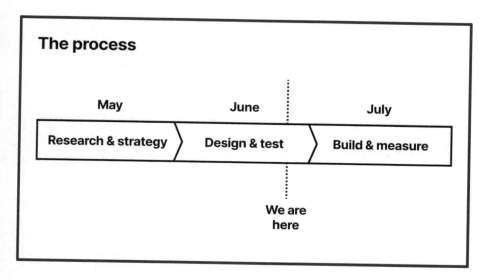

Show these phases one-by-one (using animations) and say *very briefly* what each phase was for. For example:

SAY » (when showing 'Research & strategy') "We spent the first three weeks clarifying what the business goals and KPIs for this work were, and we also spent time with users understanding their needs and challenges. (Show the next phase, 'Design & test') Recently we've been in the 'Design & test' phase, hence this meeting, which leads me to today's purpose."

Why this meeting

The purpose of your meeting will depend on your situation. Let's cover a few of the most common reasons for high-stakes design presentations.

Reason 1: alignment

These meetings update stakeholders about progress so other teams are aware of your work and how it might affect them. In this situation, there's usually an unspoken rule: if they don't like something, or it doesn't fit their strategy, stakeholders can challenge the work. So your true task is *alignment,* making sure everyone understands and accepts the direction you're proposing.

> **SAY »** "We're excited today to show you our latest thinking about this work. Today we'd like to ensure all of you are up to date on our progress and aligned with where we are going."

Today's purpose

Alignment

Reason 2: gather input

If you're seeking expert input (you should always do this anyway!) you might like to make that explicit, too. If stakeholders are left out of the process, or if you genuinely need help deciding on the direction of the work, your explicit goal might be to gather input.

> **SAY »** "We've explored several directions to this work, but we need your help. Today we'd like to gather your input to help us decide the right course of action."

Reason 3: approval

If you work in one of those slightly slower, hierarchical organisations that requires sign-off on all the work, then be explicit about it.

> **SAY »** "As we are close to the end of the design process and are about to start building the first version of the product, we are here today to update you on our progress and get your approval to proceed."

Sometimes you're looking for approval on something more specific than an entire feature or product, e.g. the navigation or a UI that matches the new brand. When this is the case, it's helpful to show a list of the things that need sign-off. This sets a helpful boundary upfront about what you need the stakeholders to approve in the meeting.

All of the above reasons for the meeting tend to bleed into each other. But by explicitly stating a single purpose, you signal what the meeting is for. When the purpose is not clear, it's easier for later conversations to drift in the wrong direction.

TASK » Make a note of your 'Why this meeting' in your outline.

The attention-grabber: use a surprising quote, quiz, or story to engage your audience

Good movies, books, or TV shows often begin by grabbing your attention, so you're compelled to keep watching. Amongst other strategies, they do this using novelty (*"Show me something I've never seen before"*), mystery (*"have to know what the big secret is!"*), or curiosity (*"That's unusual, tell me more!"*).

Good stories need to wake us up a bit, and draw us in. People are usually reluctant to use these methods in the business world because they seem irrelevant or unserious. But they are a blessed relief amongst the boring, day-to-day business fluff. You can also use the attention-grabber to put your audience in the right frame of mind for what comes later.

How? A good attention grabber can come in many forms, but here are a few of the go-to methods you should consider in order of the difficulty it takes to come up with them, from easy to hard.

Quotes (easy)

The right quote can set the scene for the rest of your presentation. If a theme underpins the story you're trying to tell, a quote on that theme is an excellent framing device. There are different types of quotes you can use.

Wisdom quote: Let's say you have stakeholders who are not familiar with the practice of design research, and you need to warm them up to the idea that it will improve decision-making. Here's a quote you can open with:

SAY » "Einstein said something interesting once…" (Switch to this slide and give them a moment to read the quote)

> # If I had only one hour to save the world, I would spend fifty-five minutes defining the problem, and only five minutes finding the solution.
>
> ## — Albert Einstein

SAY » "On this project, we decided to take some inspiration from someone far smarter than ourselves! Because there are a lot of differing opinions around the business about what this product should be, we wanted to de-risk our decisions. We've spent a lot of time understanding the problems our users face, and we are now much more confident that this product will be a success."

You've got their attention, you've appealed to a higher authority, and you've explained your research-led approach. Look for quotes that are thought-provoking, ones that will make people think and pay attention.

TIP » To find a good quote, refer to books or articles you've found helpful to your profession. You can also identify the theme you want to highlight and search for quotes about it.

'Voice of the user' quote: One of your more accessible sources of inspiration is your users. Nothing helps people to understand the challenges in your design work more than listening to users. Keep your ear to the ground for interesting highlights in what users say. Look for quotes with one or more of these qualities:

- Surprising – it helps you see the work in an unexpected light
- Funny – it will make people laugh, or at least smile
- Insightful – a non-obvious, deeper truth about the work

SAY » "When I was interviewing users who stopped using our service, here's what someone said:"

> **You know, when you have dietary needs like mine, sometimes it feels like you're the runt of the litter! All you get is leftover scraps.**
>
> **— Vegan user**

SAY » "This is who we should be aiming for! Let's turn a user who feels they're a neglected runt into an equal member of the family whose needs matter as much as anyone else's."

You don't need to be lucky to find quotes like this. When you've done your homework by talking to users, you can usually find something that will help people understand their mindset and grab your audience's attention.

TIP » Scan your research findings for the shortest, most concise quote that captures what users need or the pains they're experiencing.

Micro-quiz (medium)

Another method of gaining attention from stakeholders is to play a little quiz with them. Take something a little bit surprising or counterintuitive and frame a question around it.

SAY » "Before we get into the body of today's presentation, let's play a little guessing game. We've been testing how we present tempting new food options to users. Which one do you think converted better: showing a dish, or showing a restaurant just with a photo of that dish?"

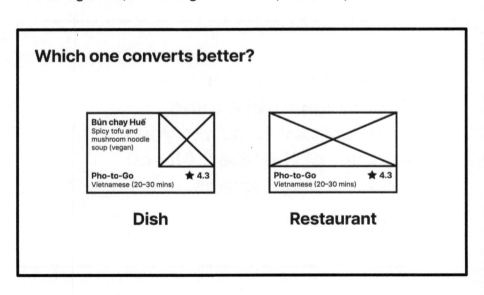

Let them guess, then reveal the answer. Questions like this get them engaging with the topic and thinking like a designer right at the start of the presentation.

TIP » Creating a good quiz question is a little design challenge. Start by finding something unexpected or surprising and build plausible questions and answers around it, making the true answer harder to spot. Ensure that the question doesn't make anyone feel silly for guessing the wrong answer.

A framing story (hard)

Many professional speakers will open their talks with a short fable or framing story, one that grabs attention from the start and helps the audience understand the themes being addressed later. Here's a story that helps people understand the potential of UX design.

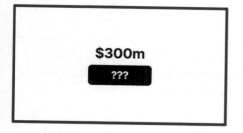 

SAY » "Ever heard the $300m dollar button story?[6] Jared Spool tells the story of how, at his firm UIE, they discovered that one button in the checkout of an ecommerce store was causing a $300m dollar annual loss in revenue. Would anyone like to guess the word on that button?"

Pause and let them guess. Then reveal the answer.

SAY » "It was 'Register.' It turns out, that when they usability-tested the checkout, people just didn't want to sign up for an account at that moment, they just wanted to finish ordering their stuff. They said things like this:"

I'm not here to be in a relationship.
— A user

SAY » "The team moved the registration process to after the checkout, and, surprisingly, most people still completed signup, and the company made an extra $300m per year. I tell this story because small changes to the UI (like a single button) can have an outsize effect on business outcomes. Later I'm going to show you some examples where we think the same thing is happening."

Stories that connect to something important about your work can be hard to find, but when they work well, they are the most effective attention-grabbers.

TIP » Don't hesitate to tell other people's stories, as long as you credit them. Presenting in private isn't an originality contest (presenting in public is a different story). Collect useful stories from podcasts, books, or elsewhere throughout your career, and re-use them when they're relevant.

Humour (hard)

What's the funniest thing that happened during the design process? It might be something that happened in a usability test you caught on video or a quote like "I'm not here to be in a relationship".

Your funny attention-grabber doesn't always need to be laugh-out-loud, but it should be relatable. Know your audience, test the material first, and keep things tasteful. A good one won't feel too forced or 'on the nose'.

ALEXA, BORE ME TO DEATH

I was once running a usability test on a voice product that was too slow, and during one session I noticed that the participant was visibly bored. While waiting for Alexa to respond, she would stare into space, sigh, or check her nails. I edited these moments together to make a funny montage video, and I prefaced it by saying, "I know people are aware the product is too slow, but today I'm going to show you why it's so important to fix this. Let's see how users feel." The video had exactly the effect I needed. All the stakeholders and engineers who had previously been ignoring this problem laughed at the montage, feeling the absurdity of having to wait over and over again. They didn't feel defensive, which they might have if they hadn't been able to laugh at the result of their own decisions.

TIP » If the content you're presenting runs counter to the organisation's way of thinking, then humour is the best way to help decision-makers swallow a bitter pill. It is much easier to accept an uncomfortable truth when you're laughing about it.

TASK » Put 'Attention Grabber' into your outline. You don't need to choose one right away if it's not obvious what will work. You can come back to it later after you have a clearer sense of what you'll be presenting and the story you'll be telling.

TIP » Many professional speakers keep a bank of attention-grabbers that they reuse over the course of many different talks. Start developing yours.

Principles: explain how you approached the design

Sometimes, stakeholders aren't familiar with how we think. Help people understand the principles behind your approach by making them explicit. If your stakeholders already understand these ideas, skip this section.

Principle

Inspiration over information

SAY » "When we were researching the way users browse our site, we realised that while the product pages had all the right information on them, they weren't very inspiring. So this became our mantra for the redesign."

Imagine that you showed a stakeholder this new design without the context of the guiding principle. You might easily dismiss the new product descriptions as 'fluffy', or the product photography as 'over-the-top'. But now that they know why you made these decisions, they're much more likely to accept something that pushes the business in a new direction.

TIP » You don't need to share all your principles. But it's a good idea to identify those that are critical for your stakeholders' understanding of the work and introduce them before you start talking about the design.

Share your insights: show what you learned, not your process

To make your stakeholders' eyes glaze over with boredom, presenting a detailed section about your design process usually does the trick. This habit may come from design education, where it is vitally important to show how you used a process to reach your insights.

But in the world of work, the balance is different. No one cares how you do your job, and the same is true for everyone else. The CEO doesn't have to explain the process of being a CEO. Engineers don't show you how they code. So although there are sometimes good reasons to show some 'how' (for example, where your research insights came from), you don't need to share nearly as much as most designers assume. More detail is not more persuasive: aim for quality over quantity.

Show the results of your process, not so much *how* you did it. What were the conclusions you reached from user research? What did you find out that has the biggest influence on the design work? How concise can you be when you explain these insights? Do this by reducing the results of your work down to snappy headlines that summarise your insights for quick and easy understanding.

Let's compare bad and good examples.

Bad example: pointless process

User interviews

Who?

- 15 new users
- Age 25 – 40
- Medium income, city dwellers
- 50% M/F

How?

- 45-min paid interviews
- Paid $50 each
- Incentive > interview > demo

Findings

Vegans can't easily find options for their diet.

But... vendors aimed at a particular diet (eg all-vegan burger joint) are growing.

80% of the time, people order the same thing from their favourite places.

The conversation about what to order often starts with a category: "what kind of food should we eat?"

New choices are often made because of attractive imagery.

Sides and options create a lot of friction in the process, ie after the main choices.

ETA on delivery is the main reason people change their mind about an order.

Most takeout options can't be browsed by food preferences.

DON'T SAY » "During the discovery phase, we interviewed twelve users for forty-five minutes each time. We recruited a mixture of ages. Some were existing users, some ex-users. We used a new recruitment agency and were very happy with the participants we got. We began with an introduction to the research..." (proceeds to talk at length through each finding).

Why this is bad:

- **No memorable headline:** just a forgettable description of this phase of work

- **Process is mostly irrelevant:** too much detail about the process, in both what is said and shown

- **Findings aren't insights:** so what if the vegans can't find options for them. What's new? The focus should be on expressing "and what does that mean for our design?"

- **Findings are buried:** by listing key findings all on one screen, they lose their power

- **Too much on one screen:** the audience will read the slide, instead of listening to you

Good example: a concise insight

Let's tighten this up using a simple rule: *one idea per slide.*

Insight #1

'Options' aren't optional
for users with dietary requirements

"I have to select the no-meat option again and again; it's like the app has amnesia."

SAY » "Before we started designing, we interviewed some potential users, and we learned that people with dietary needs (like vegans) spend much more effort finding and selecting their options every time they come back. They aren't really 'options' if you think about it; they're requirements. If we want to serve this growing market, we must learn their preferred food options, and personalise the experience so it's less work to get what you need." (reveal quote)

Why this is good:

- **Memorable headline:** crucial context for the design choices you are going to show later

- **Focussed and concise:** the slide is about one thing only and is low on detail

- **Evocative:** the quote and photo of a real person solidify the insight with some easy-to-understand evidence

Reduce your research down to one key fact you want to communicate and summarise how this impacts your design. Do *not* go into detail about your methodology without good reason. Most stakeholders will trust you did the right thing, and if they need to verify, they can do so during the Q+A session at the end of the presentation.

When the 'how' matters

People need to know only as much 'how' as necessary to accept that you know what you're talking about. But *sometimes*, you might need to say a little bit more about your methods.

Representative research subjects: Many stakeholders like to know that you've done your research with users who represent the product's actual market. Give them a little bit of reassurance that your research was rigorous by explaining briefly whom you recruited.

Unexpected or challenging findings: When you discover something unexpected or that runs contrary to what people already think, it's important to spend more time explaining how you discovered these facts, as they are more likely to be challenged. In this situation, you may need to play the scientist and explain in more detail why you've reached the conclusions you have. The best strategy is triangulation. Show you have multiple sources (e.g. qualitative and quantitative data) for your findings. Tell a story, but back it up with numbers.

For maximum persuasion, show something real that people can empathise with, like an interview or video clip. For example, I once worked with one retail organisation who had a hard time believing that the in-store signage wasn't working well. We filmed people with mobility challenges struggling to use the stairs because they'd missed the sign to the elevator. We included quotes from these users about how hard it was and measured how many people missed the sign in a single day.

Collaboration and consultation: When you've worked closely with colleagues (for example in other departments) in your process, then you should explain the collaboration and give credit where it's due.

Avoid presenting too many insights

Let's say you found ten themes in your research. Should you present all ten? Absolutely not. Reduce the key findings down to ones more relevant to the story you will tell—four or five is fine. You can share the rest in a document after the meeting, should anyone need it.

TASK » Put 'Research Insights' into your outline, along with some headline items. You don't have to get these word-perfect right now at the outlining stage. Just capture a few ideas and themes.

CHAPTER 4

Structure part II: show the design through a story

In this chapter you'll outline the second half of your presentation—the story of someone using your design—and then give people the chance to offer feedback and ask questions.

Warnings and caveats: avoid nasty surprises

If you're going to present something unexpected to your audience or if you need them to take something specific into consideration while assessing your design, clarify this before you show any design work. If nothing needs a warning or a caveat, skip this step.

Heads up...

Warnings

Let's say you've deviated from the brief. You're going in an unexpected direction outside of the brand guidelines, but with good reason. Tell people that upfront before you show any work. That way, when they see it, they won't be surprised or confused. Spoilers are useful if you need to make a movie a little less shocking.

SAY » "Before we see any of the work, I need to let you know that our new design is a bit different from the existing brand. Through our research we recognised an opportunity to celebrate diverse dietary needs, and we've updated the look and feel to reflect that. We want the brand to feel relevant to those in the market who have traditionally been overlooked."

Caveats

Sometimes you might present unfinished or low-fidelity work (e.g. the wireframes). Explain what this means before they see screens, *especially* when stakeholders aren't too familiar with UX design methods.

SAY » "Before we look at any of the screens, I need to give you some context about the stage we're at. Today we are signing off the UX that we're proposing. That means you'll be looking at wireframes. These are prototypes of the final product without the finished branding or imagery. So today we'll be discussing how the design works, we won't be discussing what it looks like."

TASK » If you feel there's something your stakeholders should know before they see your designs, add 'Warnings and Caveats' to your outline.

Frame the feedback: explain what's useful and what's not

You need to tell your stakeholders what kind of feedback is useful to this discussion. The clearer you can be about what you need and what you don't, the greater your chance of successful collaboration. You also need to manage how feedback will occur. This will be different depending on whether the presentation is remote or in-person and the size of the audience.

So frame the feedback process before they see the design. Many ideas and questions will pop into their heads while they see it. If they can identify unhelpful feedback that pops into their head before they even get to say it, everyone saves time.

What feedback

To guide people into giving you better input, show them a slide with examples of good and bad feedback.

SAY » "To get the most out of your input today, I'd like to frame the kind of feedback that's most helpful to us. I know you're going to have a lot to say about the design, so follow these guidelines to help us make it even better!"

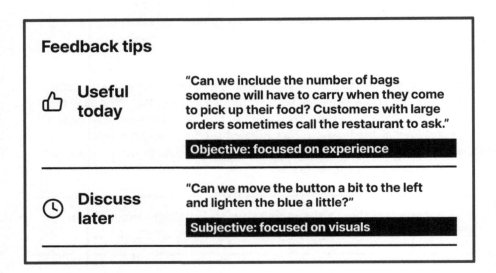

SAY » "This first example is good feedback to us because it's objective, not a personal opinion, and speaks to the customer's desired experience. Since we're reviewing UX today, we don't need to discuss how the product looks. That comes later. If you see something that's not to your taste, let's discuss after this meeting one-on-one."

Remember that humans gonna human. When they see your design, they will have a whole bunch of thoughts, and you can't control whether they share them, even if you provide warnings and caveats. Don't let this derail your efforts. This section won't stop people from giving unhelpful feedback or suggestions, it will just nudge them a little bit in the right direction. And during any later conversation, you can refer to these feedback tips.

Manage how and when stakeholders give feedback

If the group consists of eight or more people, limit the conversation to the allocated discussion time.

> **SAY »** "There are quite a few people here today, so in order to respect everyone's time, I ask that you make a note of any questions you have as I present, and we can discuss them towards the end."

For smaller groups, it's not as important to limit questions to the Q&A if you want to allow people to ask them as they come up. Later we'll discuss how to use a moderator and timekeeper to make sure that no part of the conversation goes on for too long.

If you are running a remote presentation, you must carefully manage the group so people don't talk over each other.

For small remote groups, where you don't mind questions along the way, use an agreed signal to have people talk.

> **SAY »** "If you'd like to ask me something along the way, please use the 'raise hand' feature."

For larger remote groups, limit questions and input to the chat feature. Read and respond to them during a set time.

> **SAY »** "As there are so many of you today, please put your questions and comments in the chat as we go along. I will respond to each one after I've finished the presentation."

TASK » Add 'Frame the Feedback' to your outline.

The scenario: describe who is using the design and why

It's story time! It can feel a little awkward at first to show design this way. But if people understand why, they will go along with you. We're going to focus this story on a single 'happy path,' the most common journey for the target users. Usually, you're *not* going to present all the journeys you've been designing for because there's not enough time to do them justice. If they come up, defer the conversation until after the meeting.

> **SAY »** "I could just show you the design today, but it's important that we put it into a little context, so you understand how people use it. Just showing you the design and getting your feedback is a bit like judging the food by looking at it instead of tasting it. I'm going to tell the story of someone using it so that you fully understand the decisions we made."

Now, we set the scene. Who is the hero, what's their situation, and what problem are they solving? We need:

A first name
Choose a name that's relatively easy to remember, say out loud, and represents your users. You must strike a balance with representation. Don't alienate your stakeholders by choosing something so unusual that they might find your story implausible ("Agamemnon, really?"), but more importantly, don't go so generic, your character becomes a cliché ("a white man named Dave, surely not?").

A photo
It's better to use photography that's not too polished. I'd rather have a photo of a user in a usability test any day over a stock photo. We're emphasising realism here, so avoid anything that's distracting or lacks credibility.

A story scenario

We will use two elements from our story ingredients—character and conflict—and condense them down into a scenario of no more than a hundred words.

For example:

> **SAY »** "Madeline is a dentist a few years into her career. After a busy week at the clinic, she sometimes orders takeout on a Friday night. She often experiences choice-paralysis when using food delivery apps, unable to find things that suit her vegan diet, at a time when she's tired and wants things to be quick and easy."

Note how simple this is. We are not dwelling on too many details about Madeline (nothing approaching persona-level detail), only what is pertinent to the story we're about to tell and the key problem we've decided to solve. In this example, the problem is that *choice is hard at a time when we should make it easy.*

TASK » Add 'Scenario' to your outline. Don't worry if you haven't articulated yours yet. You can come back to it later.

The story: show your hero using the design

This is the most important part of your presentation. To tell this story, you must outline it in more detail. You should decide which parts of the design you will talk about in-depth (the highlights) and which you will skim (the lowlights).

Choose your highlights with care

As with all good storytelling, you must be selective about which 'scenes' you are choosing to highlight; you can't go into detail about everything. Skim through the parts of low importance (like logging in) and slow down on the key parts of the experience.

The mundane, skimmable lowlights will usually outnumber your highlights. Ask yourself these questions to identify the important parts of the story:

- Where is a user making the key decisions or actions?
- What order allows me to tell a good story about the expected behaviours?
- Which parts are most likely to affect business outcomes?
- Which parts of the experience require the most effort?
- Which ones will the stakeholders care most about?

Planning your highlights

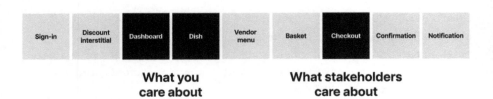

That last one deserves extra consideration. Stakeholders aren't always aware of which screens are most relevant to the objectives you're interested in. Make screens they care about highlights, even if you diplomatically explain why they're less critical than they think. **Which** elements are lowlights will depend on your design. For one product, the login screen may be non-critical to performance. For others, it may be the very thing that you're trying to improve.

Also look at the flow of the story, as per the advice in chapter one. Make sure that the story you're telling is glued together by **'therefore'** (compelling story) rather than **'and then'** (a sequence of events). Explain why your user is making certain critical choices along the way. Now let's look at how to present them, starting with how **not** to.

TASK » Map your highlights and lowlights of the user journey.

How not to present a design

Many design presentations go sideways not because there is anything wrong with the design, but because a stakeholder's attention is drawn to things that aren't pertinent to the discussion. Design work is often presented by showing an entire screen. Stakeholders get distracted when they see this because they're not in the same mindset as a user. Their head fills up with questions about everything. Why this colour? Why that image? What does that navigation item lead to? The list goes on, from the sensible to the aesthetically ridiculous ("can you make the shark's nose less pointy?").

In contrast, users typically hunt for signs they recognise that help them complete their task: they filter out everything that seems irrelevant. The context in which stakeholders and users process a design could not be more different. Here's an example of what happens in stakeholders' minds when you reveal an entire screen:

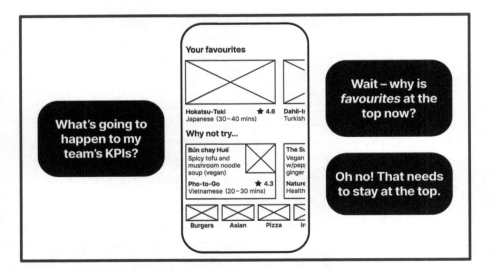

Showing them the whole screen is like asking someone to find a specific book in a wide-angle photo of a library: seeing the whole thing doesn't help. Instead, manage the audience's attention with care. When a magician sneaks a card up their sleeve, they make sure the audience is looking elsewhere. Fortunately, you don't need to be nearly as sneaky. The best method is absurdly simple: show things you want to talk about right now and hide things you don't.

This applies both to *which parts* of a design you want to talk about, but also *which fidelity.* In the examples below, we reveal the UI design at the end after we made sure that stakeholders understood the expected behaviour by looking at wireframes. We separate the moment at which people understand the function from the moment at which they judge the form.

Slow down for the highlights

You will slow down time on the highlight sections, and you'll break down how the user will experience them in much more detail. This is where your rationale gets explained. Why did you make the choices you did? Your storytelling will put stakeholders into the mindset of the user. You'll take several minutes to explain complex interactions that might only take a few seconds to complete in real-time, like the slow-motion bullets in

The Matrix. This lets you explain your rationale in detail. For example, as someone scans down the screen browsing products.

You will cover:

- what the user is thinking and feeling
- what they are doing
- your rationale for your choices
- what outcomes this produces

You slow down time by:

- directing the attention of your audience
- revealing the design step-by-step

Let's take a highlight from our food-delivery app design and use these methods to present one important screen.

NOTE » In these examples, you'll see a layer covering the parts of the design we don't want stakeholders to see yet. Start by covering the entire screen, and reveal slowly, using animations where possible.

SAY » "Madeline has just got home from work, crashed into the sofa, and opened the app to order some dinner. She's tired and isn't in the mood to think too hard about what to order. But she also feels like she should eat something a little healthier than her favourites. 70% of our returning customers order the same things repeatedly, so we want to make sure Madeline sees her favourites first."

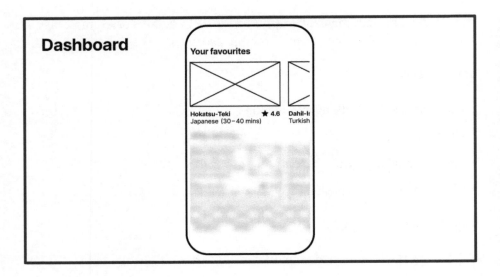

Dashboard

Your favourites

Hokatsu-Teki ★ 4.6 Dahil-I:
Japanese (30–40 mins) Turkish

SAY » "One difference to note here is that the items in this favourites list are restaurants she's ordered from before, not dishes. People tend to re-order a few things from one place when they're looking for something familiar. As she scans down to the next section, 'Why Not Try...', she sees something a little different: dishes."

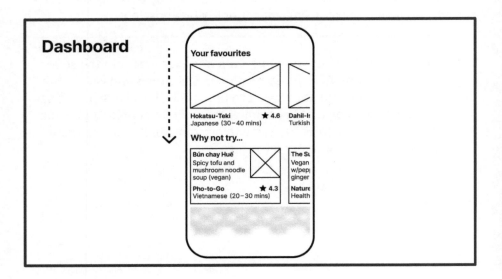

Dashboard

Your favourites

Hokatsu-Teki ★ 4.6 Dahil-I:
Japanese (30–40 mins) Turkish

Why not try...

Bún chay Huế The Su
Spicy tofu and Vegan
mushroom noodle w/pep|
soup (vegan) ginger

Pho-to-Go ★ 4.3 Nature
Vietnamese (20–30 mins) Health

SAY » "Madeline is now looking at best-selling vegan dishes from restaurants she hasn't tried yet. She's never told the app that she's vegan. We just learned it over time from her orders. This offers her attractive and relevant choices. In our testing, we learned that when you're feeling like trying something new, showing new dishes worked better than showing new restaurants."

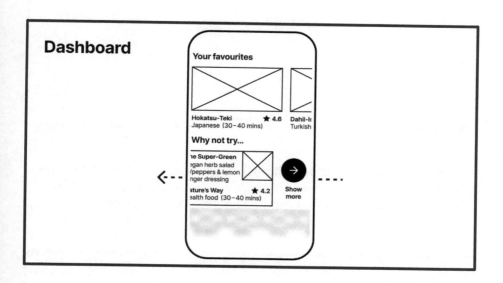

SAY » "Madeline is curious about the items on this list because it feels magically relevant, and the images are enticing. But as horizontal scrolling feels a little awkward after a while, we've put a 'show more' link after 10 or so items. She's feeling very tempted by some of these dishes, but she's not done exploring the dashboard options."

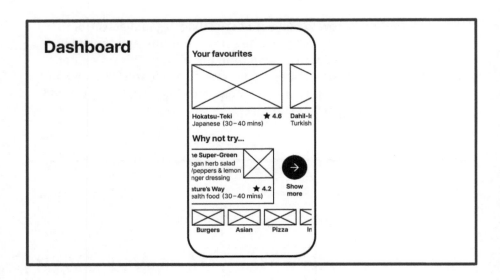

SAY » "Now we reach the traditional category options. If Madeline did have a specific type of food on her mind, they are easily accessible here. She takes a brief look out of habit, but nothing grabs her."

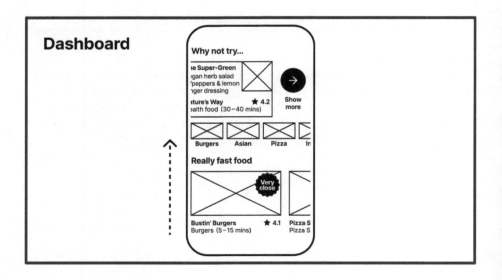

SAY » "We've also learned that at particular times of the week, people often order what's fastest to deliver. Madeline sees a few restaurants that are close to her apartment and have fast preparation times. Notice that we've changed the emphasis of the estimated delivery time to reassure people that they will get really fast food. Madeline scrolls back up to 'Why Not Try'. She's noticed a couple of really tempting new dishes but wants to see a few more before deciding for sure. She taps 'see more' and moves on to the full list."

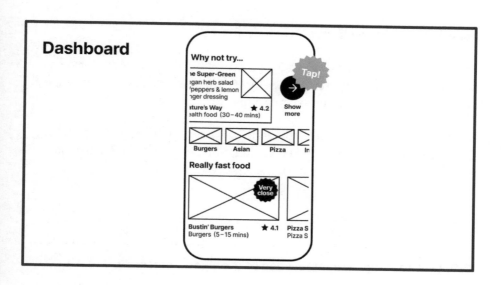

| **SAY »** "Let's have a look at this design in hi-fidelity."

SHOW » Final high-fidelity UI design.

SAY » "Before we go further, let me just say that this design and this order of items on the dashboard has been extensively tested already. Our A/B testing showed a 3% potential uplift in conversion, and we've had lots of positive comments when we've watched people using it. In fact, let me show you a video now."

SHOW » Short video clip of someone using this screen from a successful usability test.

Going into this level of detail for a highlight may seem a tad much, but this effort is what will ensure a high level of shared understanding between everyone in the room.

Speed up for the lowlights

For whichever elements of your design are non-critical to your story (e.g. fly-out navigation, login screens, or interstitials), show how they'll be used but avoid lengthy reveals or explanations of the rationale.

In our example lowlight of a login screen, it needs to be a part of our story for continuity, but it doesn't need explanation because it's not a critical piece of the user experience in this scenario.

I   **SAY »** "Madeline logs in…"

SHOW » A sped-up, animated video of the sign-in process.

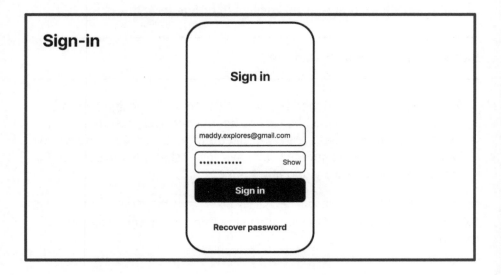

Outcomes: give your story a happy ending for the user and the organisation

Once you've taken the stakeholders through the story, you need to end on a high note, calling back to The Why—the purpose of this work. The ending should contain these elements:

1. **The user outcome**: How has your design helped the user overcome the challenge they faced? Was it easier than the existing product? What needs were met by this journey? How did the user feel?

> **SAY »** "Madeline chooses a healthy meal to be delivered, and 20 minutes later she's discovering new flavours that she loves. To summarise: thanks to the changes in our design, Madeline used our app to discover food that perfectly suited her diet at a time in her week when finding the right thing is usually a chore, especially for vegans."

2. **The business objective**: what business needs were met by this journey?

> **SAY »** "Because we helped her find the right thing quickly, Madeline chose our service when she was getting a little tired of the old

favourites. Our conversion rate goes up, as does customer satisfaction and retention."

Our objective

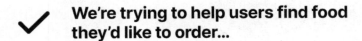 **We're trying to help users find food they'd like to order...**

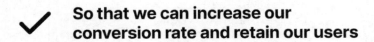 **So that we can increase our conversion rate and retain our users**

This ending explicitly calls back to the 'whys' at the beginning of your presentation. This is your conclusion, your *raison d'etre*. The entire story must lead to the outcomes and ambition in your original 'why'.

TASK » Add 'Outcomes' to your outline.

Discussion: questions, comments, and answers

Later in this book, we will tackle the tricky subject of dealing with stakeholder discussions, as that conversation deserves its own chapter. But for now, while creating an outline, all you need to do is plan what kind of feedback session you will have.

SAY » "Thanks for listening. We'd like to gather your input on this now. In this discussion I'd ask two things of everyone. First, let's keep this impersonal. This is about the design, not the designer. Second, let's avoid solutionising. We can talk about what's working and what's not,

| but it's better if we don't try to design the thing during this meeting."

That last point is hard to stick to for many stakeholders, but at the very least, you've defined what healthy discussion sounds like.

Give people time to capture their thoughts

You'll get much better feedback if you give people some thinking time to process what's on their minds. In addition, we'll prompt them to think about the positives, so the feedback discussion isn't purely negative.

> **SAY »** "I'd like to ask you now to take a few minutes to write down three things you think are working well in the design, and three things you have comments or questions about.
>
> We've sent you a link to the design just now in case you want to take a closer look while you reflect." (This can also be a printed handout).

The discussion format

Now you open the discussion. What you do here depends on the formality, setting (remote vs. in-person), and the size of audience.

Reflection time   **(5m, on your own)**

Write down three things you like about the design, and three things you'd like to give feedback on.

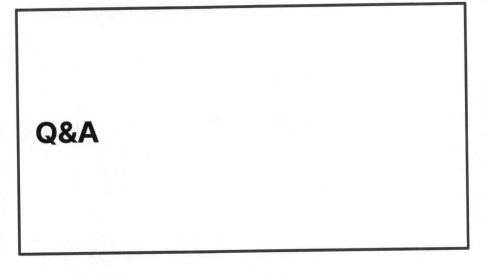

Q&A

Small groups (less than 8 people): open discussion

You can invite open discussion for small groups. You'll still need to keep an eye on time and ensure that everyone gets heard, but you don't need to moderate as much as you do with larger groups.

SAY » "Thanks for listening. I'd love to hear what you think, and I'm here to answer any questions you have."

Medium-sized groups (8-15): turn-taking

You *can* have an open discussion, but a conversation of this size is challenging to manage. Instead, use moderated turn-taking to ensure everyone gets to contribute.

SAY » "I'd love to hear your comments and questions, I know you've been noting things down. To make sure we've heard from everyone, I'll just go round the group one-by-one, but don't feel obliged to say anything if you don't want to."

Now you go around the group allowing people to ask questions or give feedback, one-by-one.

Large groups (15+): moderated Q+A

There's simply no way to have productive open discussions with so many people in the audience. This needs to be a Q+A, not an open discussion, and you need to moderate carefully.

In-person

> **SAY »** "We have 15 minutes for Q+A now. Please raise your hand if you have something to share. If we don't get to your question, please capture it on a post-it, and we'll respond afterwards."

Now you can choose who to respond to. If there are senior stakeholders who might feel particularly entitled to give feedback, you need to make sure they are heard without letting them drown out other voices.

Remote

Ask people to write their questions into the meeting chat, or perhaps into a remote collaboration tool. Then take the time to scan through these questions and pick ones to respond to. If there are too many, it's worth choosing questions and comments either a. from senior stakeholders who expect to be heard, and b. those questions most pertinent to the discussion.

Allocate one-third of the time to discussion

When planning how long you need for Q+A, a general rule of thumb is to use around one-third of your total time for the meeting. So if you have one hour, plan for 15-20 minutes of discussion, or 20-30 mins for a 90-minute meeting. It's always good to err on the side of caution and leave more time for it than you think you need.

Of course, there's no perfect amount of time to deal with all the issues and questions that might arise in every situation. You (or a colleague) have to moderate the discussion so you stick to time and make sure everyone is heard, however much time you use.

TASK » Add 'Feedback' to your outline and make a note of which format is most appropriate to your situation.

Close the meeting: make the next steps explicit

To bring the meeting to a satisfying conclusion, it's important to include some easily overlooked housekeeping.

Thank yous

Thank people for their time and input. Even when you're facing difficult criticism, it's important to show gratitude. Note that this isn't an admission that every piece of feedback was useful, or that you will act on it. It's simply a way to acknowledge that your stakeholders' input is a part of the process.

> **SAY »** "I just want to thank everyone for their time and input today. While we may not all agree on every point, we were seeking diverse viewpoints on this work as a way of sense-checking it, and you really helped us do that."

What's next

Make it clear what's going to happen next, who is doing it, and when.

Sharing the presentation

Let people know that you're going to send them a version of your slides so that they can refer to them if needed.

Further discussion

If you'd like further discussion or feedback to take place in a particular tool or format, remind them how to do it, e.g. with a link that you'll send with the slides. Whatever format you're using to share the designs and presentation, it helps when people can leave comments about the design while they're looking at it. Use whatever tools are at your disposal to make commenting available to them *in context*; for example, a web-based collaborative design tool.

Process

If there is a major milestone coming next, make it clear (perhaps by re-using your Status Reminder slide).

Actions, deferrals and follow-ups

If any actions were decided in the meeting, repeat them here so people leave knowing what they need to do. Don't be afraid to defer on discussions and tasks. It's not always possible to resolve disagreements and discussions in the time you have. Use the promise of a one-on-one follow-up to avoid rabbit-hole discussions—and make sure they happen.

TASK » Add 'Closing' to your outline and make note of what to include.

You should now have a rough outline of your presentation structure on sticky notes and a good idea of why you should include each section. My template outline isn't intended to be definitive for all situations: your story may need more, less, or something a little different.

TIP » If you're *not* iterating the outline or removing items before you jump into creating content, that's a sign that you're not thinking hard enough about your story. A good outline is usually the result of judicious revision of the order and the content. For example, updating the generic placeholder titles with real ones where possible. This process will likely continue as you write, design, and rehearse the presentation.

CHAPTER 5

Writing: sharpen your rationale with well-crafted words

Now it's time to write and edit what you will say in your presentation. In this chapter, we'll explore shortcuts to make writing easy.

> When first designing something, getting caught up in the details is easy. But once you try explaining what you're building to someone else, you must distill down what's essential and how everything fits together to make sense of it.[7]

— Tanner Christensen, Designer at Netflix, Lyft, Facebook

Writing requires taking a loose, complex set of ideas and summarising them clearly and concisely. This is difficult for many designers: we generally prefer pixels to prose. Crafting your words before designing the presentation is tough at first, but it pays off in ways that aren't immediately obvious because...

Writing is thinking.
Writing and editing will force you to think more clearly about what you're trying to communicate. It is much harder to bullshit a reader than it is a listener. Writing your talk, instead of improvising it on the day, will force you to be clearer about what you are saying. As bestselling author James Clear puts it, "Writing is the antidote to confusion".[8]

Editing prevents rambling.
Editing is a form of useful constraint. Good stories stay on track, remember? It's easy to ramble on with too much detail. By writing and editing first, it will be easier for you to spot unnecessary words and sharpen the points you want to make.

Memorable headlines emerge after writing.
When your stakeholders see a slide on the screen, you want the title of that slide to capture the main idea quickly and memorably. Write first, and the memorable headline will be easier to find because writing helps you discover the concise, compelling version of what you're trying to say.

Reading out loud improves your speaking and writing.

Your goal is to become a better speaker. Actors and performers practise this by reading aloud until they sound natural, so you need to write them first. Bonus benefit: the more you practise reading written words, the less you'll come to rely on a script in any situation.

Knowing the importance of writing is one thing; doing it is another. A blank document can be an intimidating thing to stare at when you need to write, especially if you're not used to it. Fortunately, there's an easy hack to get your first draft out.

Transcribe it: get a first draft fast

Many designers aren't used to writing at length; it's something we mostly leave behind at school. But if you want to be clear, you must. Cure your natural reluctance to write by improvising the first draft of your talk and using automated transcription to capture it. Speaking your first draft ensures you won't stop to nit-pick anything. You just get all your ideas out without stopping.

Things you'll need:

- A transcription service: the dictation feature on your laptop is often good enough

- A quiet place where you won't feel self-conscious or be interrupted

- Recording software. Record the audio for a rough sense of the length

- Your outline and key designs for reference as you talk through them

---

TASK » Transcribe your first draft. Hit record or transcribe and improvise the presentation by following your outline. It will feel awkward at first, and that's OK. All you need is a messy first draft to edit; the quality doesn't matter.

Edit: use tools to make your words clear and concise

Now you've got a first draft of your talk, it's time to edit. Just like with design, you'll do multiple passes over the text: read, edit, re-read, edit, repeatedly, as if you're sharpening a knife. With the help of writing tools, you can do a good job at editing without a lot of writing experience.

The biggest challenge for designers is being concise. It is *exhausting* to listen to someone who talks in too much detail, doesn't pause, or repeats themselves. Edit your words ruthlessly. This process will reveal just how many of your spoken words can be deleted. Here's a step-by-step editing process to get your text ship-shape.

1. Assess the duration and word count

Look at the length of your draft recording: the duration you're aiming for will be around two-thirds or less of your total meeting time—for example, forty minutes for an hour-long meeting.

Calculating your WPM (words per minute) will give you a rough sense of how fast you're talking. Take the total word count from your transcription and divide it by the duration of the recording. In chapter seven you'll find further guidance on the ideal speed, but for now, note your WPM so you can compare it to your later rehearsals.

2. Read and edit: first pass (basic)

Now read and edit your transcribed text. Add placeholder headings as you go, using your outline. Start by editing any mistakes in the transcription. Remove any 'ums', 'ahs', or other filler words; fix awkward phrasing; cut repetitive, unnecessary, or incomplete sentences. Cut, cut, cut, but don't preoccupy yourself with rewriting too much just yet.

3. Use a writing aid to assess quality

After some basic editing, use an automated writing aid to improve the text further. Writing apps can help you:

- Remove jargon or complex words. This is known as "reducing the reading age". Even though your audience will be composed of professional adults, it's easier to understand something written for a wider audience.

- Improve your grammar.

- Reduce the length of sentences. Shorter sentences are easier to comprehend.

- Fix typos and spelling errors.

4. Read and edit: second pass (refine)

Next, take a scalpel to your text. Read through it again and edit with these questions in mind:

i. Does this paragraph express a single idea?
If not, break it up or cut it. For example:

> We learned that people with allergies spend an average of around 40% more time finding ~~and checking~~ the food they order to make sure it's right for them. They often have to go hunting even deeper into the food menus, sometimes even calling the restaurant after ordering, to be absolutely sure. ~~We talked to some users who enjoyed calling the restaurant and learning the names of the people working there.~~

ii. Can the same idea be communicated with fewer words?
~~We learned that~~ People with allergies currently spend ~~an average of~~ around 40% more time finding and checking the food they order to make sure it's right for them. They ~~often have to~~ go hunting ~~even deeper~~ into the food menus, sometimes even calling the restaurant after ordering to check, ~~to be absolutely sure.~~

iii. Do stakeholders need to know this?

> People with allergies currently spend around 40% more time checking the food they order to make sure it's right for them. Sometimes they ~~go hunting into the food menus, even~~ call the restaurant after ordering to check.

iv. Can you use clearer words?

Can you cut useless superlatives? (e.g. 'very', 'basically', 'great')

Can you make the details more precise? (e.g. 'mouth-watering' over 'tasty')

> People with allergies ~~currently~~ now spend around 40% more time checking the food they order to make sure ~~it's right~~ the food is safe for them. Sometimes they call the restaurant after ordering to check.

iv. Is the rationale behind your design choices well-argued?

> People with allergies now spend around 40% more time checking the food they order to make sure the food is safe for them. Sometimes they call the restaurant after ordering to check. Finding these options should be easier. For these users, it's a matter of life and death.

Editing is similar to iteration in the design process. You'll look over your work several times, making tiny adjustments along the way to perfection. You'll step away from it for a while to gain some perspective. You'll be engaged initially—and bored to tears towards the end. You'll seek feedback from others. Most of all, you'll ask yourself if the words are answering the question you've set out to answer: why is your design the way it is?

In the end, you'll have a concise and clear edit of your talk. Now you can write better headlines.

Headlines: refine to make them memorable

Finding a memorable, clear headline takes time and revision. By writing first, you'll sometimes find the headline has already written itself.

Forgettable	V1: Placeholder **Research finding #1**	This is typically what you might write when outlining and don't care about the specific words. It's just a placeholder. Be wary of leaving headlines in this state: it's easy to do but will bore your audience.
↑	V2: Theme **Allergies**	Now we are capturing the theme of the finding. We can summarise it broadly with a headline word, but we aren't explaining the issue.
Memorable ↓	V3: Headline **Users with allergies face difficult life- and-death choices**	This is the version that emerged after writing about the subject. The audience will now have a much clearer idea about the problem you're about to explain, even before you speak. They can understand what you want to say from the headline alone.

Like design elements, headlines have patterns. You can use them to generate different ways of saying the same thing. Use the methods in the table below to produce a diverse set of headlines to choose from.[9]

Method	Example	How it works
Metaphor and Simile	Like water down the drain: how we forget user preferences	Compare x to y
Personification	The amnesiac app that forgets user preferences	Make something a person
Hyperbole	Forget preferences, lose users	Exaggerate, or take it to an extreme
Parallelism	Options aren't optional	Repeat or rhyme similar concepts
The Question	Are you really a customer if we can't remember you?	Use a provocation
Turn of Phrase	Familiarity makes the heart grow fonder	Modify a saying
The Twist	We love our users (except when we forget them)	Add a surprise at the end

TIP » The true test of a headline is whether stakeholders remember it afterwards. You can conduct lightweight headline testing before the presentation, by reading a few to colleagues and then asking them to repeat them back. The ones they remember are probably better. After the presentation, you'll know you have a winner when stakeholders repeat it back to you in conversation.

TASK » Go through the draft of your talk and rewrite your key headlines where needed.

Now you've been through writing and editing, it's time to celebrate! The talk is in great shape; you've worked through the hardest phase of content creation. Here are some bonus tips.

Use The Goldilocks Zone of detail: not too much, not too little

In astrophysics, The Goldilocks Zone is the area of a solar system just the right temperature for liquid water on planets and, therefore, more likely to contain life. Not too hot (no water) and not too cold (ice); it's 'just right'.

✗ Too much	✓ Just right	✗ Too little
We learned that people with allergies spend an average of around 40% more time finding and checking the food they order to make sure it's right for them.	People with allergies now spend around 40% more time checking the food they order, to make sure the food is safe for them.	People with allergies now spend around 40% more time checking the food they order.
They often have to go hunting even deeper into the food menus, sometimes even calling the restaurant after ordering, to be absolutely sure.	It's a life-and-death situation for some, so they'll call the restaurant after ordering to double-check.	
We talked to some users who enjoyed calling the restaurant and learning the names of the people working there.		
They do this because the wrong choice is existential: eating the wrong thing could kill you. As a result, choosing food from an unfamiliar source can be an anxiety-inducing act.		
These people are often traumatised by the memories of when their allergy was triggered.		

If you're in doubt about how much to say about a topic, try writing a version that's too long, and then one that's too short. Do the *wrong* thing to find the *right* thing.

Repetition: drive your main points home with consistent wording

Listen to any of the most infamous politicians, and you'll notice something: they use catchy, repeated phrases to drive a point home. It's both a way to spread an idea, and a method of propaganda. It's not good or bad on its own; it's what you do with it that counts.

Let's say that one of your working principles is to reduce cognitive load so users spend less time confused. If you talk through the interface off the top of your head, you'll likely use different phrases to mean the same thing: "reduce cognitive load", "we've simplified that here", "this screen is less confusing", "users don't have to think too hard about this decision".

Find the simplest way of stating the concept, e.g. "reduce thinking time", and use it repeatedly and consistently throughout your talk. You'll be priming stakeholders to understand and believe in the concept's importance.

TASK » Scan your presentation text for concepts that repeat, word them clearly, and edit for consistency.

Kill your darlings: focus on the essentials by editing ruthlessly

Good stories are almost *always* the result of judicious editing. Kill your darlings: don't be afraid to remove ideas or examples you're attached to if they don't serve the story. Examine the ups and downs to make sure your story has a good shape, without long dips or boring sections. Remove, move, or shorten sections as you see fit. If you're *not* making major changes to the structure or the content, that is a sign you're not iterating enough. The amount you edit is correlated to the quality of your presentation, just like design.

You've now got a script for everything in your outline and some memorable headlines to go with them. You know your presentation is roughly the right length. Finally, it's time to do the thing you probably wanted to do first: design the presentation. The story is done. Now it's time for screens.

CHAPTER 6

Slides: design for listening, not reading

There's no linear process to follow in this chapter. You already know how to design a presentation, so use these principles to create slides that support what you will say.

Minimise words on screen to keep people listening

When you send a slide deck to someone, they'll read it. But during a presentation, they must listen *and* read, which are difficult to do simultaneously.

Prioritise listening. The most common presentation crime people commit is to fill up the screen with content. When you put words on a screen, you are making it harder for someone to listen to you. You—not the slides—are the storyteller. Therefore, minimise words on the screen, so people pay attention to you.

How many words should you show? I use three main types of slides when presenting design.

1. A text slide

Use these when making a point or beginning a new section of your presentation. Use a few words on screen to make what you're saying memorable and clear. *Maybe* add a visual flourish, like an icon, illustration, or background photo, to back it up.

You can vary text slides slightly by including things like quotes or instructions, which will often require a few more words. But the rule is one slide, one idea. This three-word example shows you just how little text you need to make an important point.

Principle

Fail Fast

2. A conceptual diagram

You need to help the audience understand an idea, so you use visual means, e.g. a sequence of events or a hierarchy. Here, use a heading, your diagram, and very few words. In the example below, the diagram does all the heavy lifting. You don't need to say much for someone to understand the concept. It should be minimal, but not so minimal that it's a mystery as to what it means.

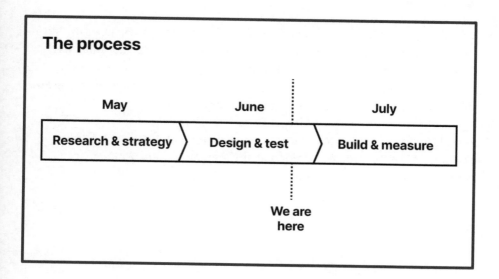

3. A design artefact

Here, you're showing stakeholders a particular design element. Use words and symbols on screen for orientation and emphasis. Reserve an explanation for the spoken word.

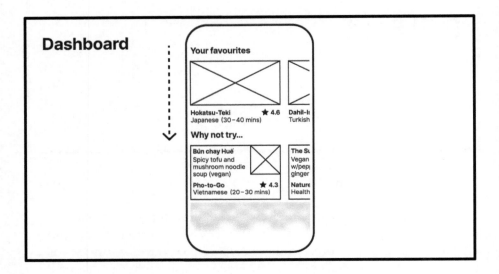

Reveal content bit by bit, so your audience doesn't jump ahead

A gradual reveal is most valuable when you're presenting the designs, but it also applies to the presentation as a whole. Diagrams, instructions, text slides: whenever there's an opportunity to match their attention to the topic you're talking about, use it. This is useful when you have more text to show on a slide: you can stop them from reading ahead.

Revealing doesn't only mean hiding, it can also mean focussing. For example, if you include the agenda at the start, highlight what you're talking about in each moment:

Today
Introduction (5m)
Research and strategy (15m)
Design (20m)
Discussion (20m)

Include sections so your audience knows where they are

A conference organiser once told me: "Half the presentations I see are largely free of structure; I don't know where I am in the talk!" Your presentation should include title slides that guide the audience through the sections of your talk, e.g. 'Research Findings', or even better, a provocative question, like: "What is challenging for users?" (which sets up your work to answer the question). Use a different slide template to signal these new sections. Use headings and subheadings together for extra-clear orientation.

TIP » Include headings, subheadings, and page numbers on every slide. Use these as signposts when sharing and referring to the slides later, which makes it easier for people to reference them.

Use variety to alleviate boredom

While all your slides should share a consistent style (and it is more efficient to create a talk using templates) some variety helps keep the audience engaged and oriented.

Colour

Create variations of your presentation's colour scheme and use them to signify sections. For example, each section can have its own text colour and background.

Layout

I keep a hand-sketched pattern library of slide layouts I've created over time close to my desk. When I know I need some variety or have trouble finding the right design, I can glance at it for inspiration.

The variety of your layouts shouldn't compromise the overall style. If you vary the layout a lot, then use consistent elements (e.g. position and typography of the slide headings).

Imagery

Creative use of sketches, icons, diagrams, notation, or photography can make vanilla slides a little more engaging and memorable.

Research and strategy

What is challenging for users?

Leave space for detail following the presentation

The minimalist approach to slide design works when you're designing for listening, but it doesn't work for people reading the presentation afterwards. They don't have all the detail you gave verbally and may have forgotten key points or context from your speech. Leave room for text in the design of your slides and add your script into the version you share with others later.

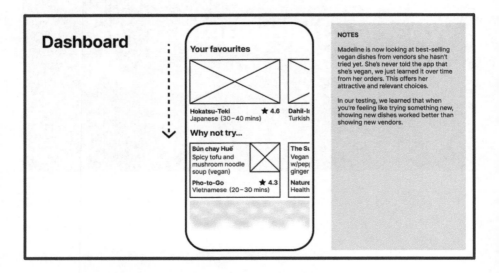

TASK » Create slides to accompany your talk.

At the end of this process, for each item in your outline, you will have a headline or heading, a paragraph (or two) for what you will say, and a slide.

Headline Max ~12 words	Options aren't optional
Paragraph Max ~100 words	Before we started designing, we interviewed some potential users, and we learned that people with dietary needs (like vegans) have to spend much more effort finding and selecting what they want, every time they come back. If we want to serve this growing market (which grew by 50% last year!), we must learn their preferred food options, and personalise the experience for those users.
Slide	

With your content done, you're now ready to rehearse the presentation.

CHAPTER 7

Rehearsal: improve your performance with feedback

In this chapter, you'll follow a rehearsal process to help you become a more confident speaker.

Find your style: confident delivery comes in many flavours

> The single most important thing to remember is that there is no one good way to do a talk. The most memorable talks offer something fresh, something no one has seen before. The worst ones are those that feel formulaic... You know what's distinctive about you and your idea. Play to your strengths and give a talk that is truly authentic to you.[10]

—Chris Anderson, curator of TED

If all talks were delivered the same way, we'd be bored watching them. TED talks may have already fallen victim to this; watch enough of them, and you'll sense the formula. Your work on the road to being a confident speaker is to learn some foundational skills that good public speakers share (like speaking clearly and at the right speed), while finding your own style. That takes experience and practice.

One of my favourite TED talks is "Stroke of Insight" by neuroscientist Jill Bolte Taylor—she explains how having a stroke deepened her understanding of the brain. It's confident and entertaining, yet Jill defies our expectations and stereotypes about what a great speaker should be. Her tone is dry. She doesn't smile much at all; if you watched it with the sound off, you wouldn't guess it's all that funny. Yet the talk is wonderful. It's surprising, educational, engaging, even spiritual, and she delivers with a clear, unassuming delivery. There are *some* common things confident speakers share. But confidence looks like a better version of ourselves, not emulating what we think confidence looks like.

Confident beats correct

Early in your career, you may feel like you have no right to decide things or speak out. You're unsure of many of your decisions and nervous about challenging anyone. Self-doubt is natural in all of us, but it is particularly acute when you're finding your feet in a new industry. The paradox is that there is no direct relationship between the level of confidence someone projects and the effectiveness of their work. You can be confidently incorrect just as much as you can be quietly correct. There's only one end of that spectrum that stakeholders respond well to though, and that's confident delivery. We unconsciously use confidence as a signpost to judge what's correct.

It's the organisation's job to make sure leaders hear the quiet voices in the room, to seek diverse opinions and not be swayed by those who speak the loudest. But since you can't control that, it's your job to grow your confidence to ensure you don't get ignored. And believe it or not, your stakeholders *want* you to be confident. They want you to tell them what to do. When stakeholders sense low levels of confidence, they try to fill it with their own. They mistake the lack of confidence in delivery for lack of confidence in the work.

Find confidence through...

1. Preparation and practice

Being prepared will give you greater confidence. You'll feel more relaxed about what you have to say, and the confidence will follow naturally. You *earned* this confidence because you worked for it. Even if you ignore the rest of the advice in this chapter, practising will boost your confidence.

2. Feedback

Feedback about how we speak can be tough to hear; it can feel like a challenge to our very identity. But because public speaking is different from everyday speech, and because it's very hard for us to perceive ourselves objectively, we need feedback to improve. In this chapter, you'll make this process a little easier by starting with self-assessment and then moving on to feedback from others.

3. Incremental improvement

No one expects you to become a confident public speaker overnight, so you shouldn't either. Find one or two things you will do differently every time you practise. Whether that's articulating words more clearly, slowing down your speech, maintaining a confident but relaxed pose, or something else, find ways to improve continually, like you do with design.

4. Fake it 'til you make it

There's less difference between fake and real confidence than most people realise. Think of it like a psychological hack; if you want to feel happier, make a point of smiling more. Act with more confidence, and you'll feel more confident. This is why performers have huddles, rituals, and pep talks before a big event; they switch themselves into performance mode. Learn a few tricks to help you with your confidence and use them.

Record yourself: find out what to improve by recording a rehearsal

Some studies have shown that the best way to start improving your public speaking is to self-evaluate.[11] Although it's awkward to listen to yourself, it's a good starting point because you can improve without the anxiety of speaking in front of others. You won't catch all the improvements you need to make, but you can solve some basics. Start by recording a short rehearsal, between five and ten minutes long.

The guidelines

- Rehearse for 5 to 10 minutes. Don't perform your complete presentation, just enough to assess your delivery.

- Use your slides as guides.

- Record video and audio. Assume the position you will be in during the actual presentation and try to record as much of your body as possible.

- Time it.

- Relax. Don't think too hard or try to 'perform'. Go for it.

Finally... read this chapter no further.

It's important that you don't bias your natural presenting style with any thought about how it *should* be done. Record yourself as you are today so you can honestly assess your delivery. Don't finish this chapter until you've done so.

TASK » Record a short rehearsal of your presentation.

Now you're ready to find improvements to your public speaking.

Self-assess the basics: speed, volume, rhythm, and expression

Before you listen to your recording, complete these tasks:

1. **Isolate the audio from your video**. Most operating systems have tools that will let you save the audio from a video as a separate file.

2. **Transcribe it**. As you did when you were writing your presentation, use a tool that will transcribe the text of your talk from the audio file. Once again, don't worry if it's not 100% accurate.

3. **Measure your WPM** (Words Per Minute). Find the word count from your transcription and divide it by the number of minutes you were speaking for to calculate the WPM.

Example calculation: 835 words / 5 mins = 167 words per minute

TASK » Watch or listen to your recording and make notes on what you observe. Once you're over the cringe factor of listening to yourself, make notes about the following qualities. Treat it like user research: observe what's happening without judgement.

Speed

The speed at which you speak (measured in WPM) strongly determines whether you will be understood. The ideal WPM for public speaking is slower than conversation, around 100-130 WPM.

Situation	Speed (WPM)
Public Speaking	100–130
Conversation	120–150
Radio and TV presenter	150–160
Auctioneer	250

It's common to start too fast because people speak more quickly when they're nervous. People also find that speaking at the right speed (more slowly) feels a little unnatural. Remember that the best speakers usually say less, with pauses for emphasis.

Rhythm and variety

We enjoy listening to actors and performers because their speech has rhythm and variety. This is even more important in public speaking because we have to listen to one person for extended periods. Good speakers leave pauses in their speech: they give our brains a few seconds to catch up with what's been said. They also vary the length of their sentences to add variety in the speech pattern.

Take Christopher Walken. Regardless of what you think about *where* he pauses when speaking (usually somewhere strange), he's interesting to listen to. A strong public speaker uses pauses to add definitive ends to sections, which add weight to their meaning. Listeners understand when a part of the story is over, or if something is important. Listen to your speech and examine the transcript with the following in mind:

Is there variety in the length of sentences? If all the sentences are lengthy, or they bleed into each other, there's something to improve.

Are there breaks and pauses? Look at the transcript while you listen. Do your pauses match the sections of the talk? Do the breaks add *weight* to the meaning? Do you notice the lengths of time between sentences or sections? Do sentences *feel* like they have endings?

Does the speed vary? If you speak at the same pace throughout, it can be a little monotonous. Good performers slow down for emphasis.

Volume

Confident speakers have a slightly elevated volume that grabs people's attention. You're not trying to reach every audience member at a theatre like an actor does, but a little bit of extra volume can help (although this matters less in smaller rooms).

So compare: is your recorded voice roughly the same volume as your conversational voice? If it is, you may need to practise being a little louder. Being too quiet is more common for women than it is for men, as society socialises boys to dominate conversations.

Repetition

Listen carefully for your habitual speech patterns. In conversation, these don't tend to matter much, but they stick out like a sore thumb when people must listen to them again and again in a longer speech.

'Ums' and 'Ahs'

These are called disfluencies. They're like glue between sentences, holding patterns while our brains catch up to what we will say next. They allow us to signal someone we're in conversation with should keep listening, that we're not done yet.

They aren't needed outside of conversation, and in public speaking, they have the unfortunate effect of making you sound a little less sure of yourself. Get comfortable with leaving silence between the things you're saying. It's a hard habit to break, but it makes a huge impact on the quality of your performance. It's one of the main differences between professional speakers and everyone else.

Habit words

We all fall into habits of speech; very few of us are aware of them. Stereotypical examples include West Coast Americans overusing the word 'like' at the start of every sentence or people using the word 'guys' to describe any group of humans (I've really struggled with that last one myself). Words like 'basically' and 'however' are often overused at the start of sentences.

Rushed or mistaken pronunciation of particular words is also a common habit. Watch out for words you rush, for example, pronouncing the word hierarchy as 'hi-ar-key' instead of 'hi-err-ar-key'.

If you listen carefully to yourself, you'll find more patterns or pronunciations unique to you. Notice your speech habits and decide whether to avoid them.

Pitch

It can be a problem because people unconsciously attribute more authority to lower voices than high ones. This unfairly advantages men with lower voices: having your ears seduced by Barry White's mellifluous bass-heavy voice is no accident.

As listeners, we should all try hard to fight this bias, but as a speaker, you can't control how aware your audience is of this problem. This is why podcasters invest in expensive, bass-capturing microphones. Chris Voss, a hostage negotiator for the FBI, called his negotiation voice "The late-night FM radio DJ tone".[12]

There are also examples of people trying too hard to lower their pitch. Convicted fraudster and Theranos founder Elizabeth Holmes deliberately modulates her natural voice a few tones lower to give herself more 'gravitas'. It sounds forced: don't do this. Just be aware of the problem and how it may affect how you're received.

Is your voice naturally higher?
Practise speaking a little slower, louder, and with clear enunciation, then

check with those you trust that it sounds natural. Try a vocal warmup exercise before you present.

Is your pitch higher, or does it wobble during a talk?
This is likely nerves. More practice and preparation will help you to feel more confident and avoid this. Use the advice in chapter ten on resilience to manage your feelings.

Tone

The effect of your tone won't be as obvious to you as when you seek peer feedback later, but you may notice some patterns that are worth examining.

For example, 'uptalk' is the habit of raising your tone at the end of a sentence. The higher sound signals uncertainty, which is why we usually do it when asking questions. Used in a statement, however, and the effects are mixed. The rising tone at the end may signal that you're questioning or disagreeing, or it may suggest you lack confidence in your answers. The danger, depending on the tone pattern and the culture you're in, is that your habitual speech is affecting your audience's interpretation of your presentation in unintentional ways. For example, surveys have shown some groups (e.g. bosses and people from the United Kingdom) consider uptalk annoying or patronising. Working in a second language is even harder. If that's you, be kind to yourself and go slow, as you have an additional challenge.

You should now have a shortlist of things you'd like to improve in your public speaking.

TASK » Summarise the improvements you need to make with short statements and put them on cards or sticky notes that are visible when you rehearse, e.g. "Slow down".

Rehearse and record a few more times so you can keep improving on the issues you've observed.

Get feedback: use peers to help you find problems you cannot see

Now it is time to invite wider feedback from peers. This is crucial because most of us are blind to how we seem to others. We spend our days looking outwards, not in the mirror, using the same old routines to talk and act. We need kind and sympathetic colleagues to give us constructive feedback.

Who to ask

Let's not underestimate how challenging this feedback might be. It's important to think about who is best placed to give you the kind of feedback you need at this stage.

Trust

The most important factor in asking for feedback is whether you trust the person. Most of us don't have the steel nerves required to gather feedback from total strangers, so we should start with people we trust to give us feedback in good faith. These are folks who care about whether we do well.

These people might be *too* kind with their feedback because they are biassed by their desire to maintain a harmonious relationship with you. But if you're starting on your public-speaking journey, start somewhere safe, perhaps with a member of your team you know well.

Positive and constructive

Think of someone who gives positive, constructive feedback. These are the people you will learn the most from. Think of the difference between someone saying:

> "You talk too fast." (pure critique)

and...

> "I think if you slow down a bit, people will understand you better." (suggestion, upheld with rationale)

If you know people who might be capable of doing the latter, you're much more likely to learn and grow from them.

Subject-neutral

You might think it's important that someone who gives you feedback on your speaking performance understands your subject matter, but at this stage it's less important than you think.

First, you're asking for feedback on your performance, not the content. So it's not *as* important that they know your subject matter.

Second, a good test for whether you're speaking clearly is whether people who aren't familiar with your subject matter still understand it. This is why you can improve your writing by reducing the required 'reading age' by leaving out complex words and overly long sentences. The better speaker you are, the more accessible and understandable you'll be, regardless of who is in the audience. Familiarity with the subject is useful later but beginning with a family member is fine.

What to present

You already made a recording, so it's fine to send it to someone for feedback. For extra bravery points, do a short talk in person. An actual performance gives you something a little more real to learn from since you're presenting in front of a live audience.

Frame the feedback

Like when you ask for feedback on designs, it's important to frame people's expectations about what kind of feedback is truly useful. First, tell them why you're doing this with them. You are seeking feedback from them because you trust them to be kind, positive, and constructive. Second, tell them that the topic isn't as important as the performance. Ask them what they notice about the clarity of your delivery. If you number your slides, this next part will be easier for them because they can write down which part of the talk their feedback relates to.

Receiving the feedback

People are naturally inclined to avoid giving critical feedback, so using a little 'good with the bad' guidance can help here. After the presentation, ask them to take a moment to write down three things they liked about your performance, and three things to improve on. This will force them to think about your challenges and have them identify which ones are important. Once they're done, get them to talk through their six items. This allows you to ask questions, like "why do you think I sound over-confident?" or "where in the talk did you notice that?"

Deciding which feedback to act on

Not all feedback is useful or equally important. Like with user research, you will need to be a little discerning about what they say. For example, "you were nodding a little too much." This is a largely useless comment that doesn't much affect how a talk is received.

"You need a little more gravitas in the way you speak." This one is common but mixed in its utility. 'Gravitas' is often used as a synonym for a deep voice. They might be telling you your voice is high, something you can't do much about. But it's important to know that this is what people perceive, so consider ways to address their feedback. For example, can you slow down or add emphasis?

"You could do with leaving bigger pauses between sections". This is the perfect feedback, an indication that you're speaking too fast or breathlessly rushing from point to point.

Physical confidence: use your face and body to engage the audience

These factors aren't as important as working on your speech (at least at first), but they can help you be a little more confident. If you filmed your rehearsals, use the following advice to look for additional improvements.

When we're feeling nervous or insecure, we'll often display it inadvertently through our body language and behaviour. We are a little quieter, our speech wobbles, we speak less clearly, avoid eye contact, and physically shrink away. Contrast this with someone who pauses briefly as they enter to greet everyone, making eye contact with the attendees. They walk at a moderate pace to their chair in a relaxed pose, holding their head high with a smile. The former is setting themselves up to be ignored, the latter to be engaged with.

For most people, this is unconscious behaviour. It's hard to see how our feelings about a meeting will affect us. Your job is to work through those feelings, fake it a little, and don't be too hard on yourself if you notice a problem. Self-consciousness inhibits us, whereas self-awareness will help you be your best self. Reframe, "Oh god, I'm rushing!" to "Huh, I'm speaking a little too fast".

Eye contact

We use eye contact in day-to-day settings to signal we are addressing someone, so there's a subtle importance to it. *Yes,* everyone knows they should be listening to you if you're the one giving a talk, but eye contact adds that little bit of extra engagement. Confident people are not afraid to make eye contact. This applies in a remote context too; people are more inclined to listen when it feels like the person is speaking directly to them. Set up your camera and screen in a way that approximates eye contact, wherever possible.

Gestures and body language

This is an entire book subject of its own, but when you're starting, it matters less than speech does. At first, just observe any obvious habits that might be a problem, like slouching, fidgeting or nervous pacing.

You've now ended up with a strong set of improvements to make to your public speaking. For some, these might be hard habits to break because they're so fundamental to who we are. That's why it's often the beginning of a journey.

Focus on slow, steady improvements as you rehearse. As designers, we often lean towards perfectionism, which can set us up for hard failures.

Instead of thinking about giving the perfect performance, think about more incremental changes. Remember that the goal of rehearsing isn't to be word-perfect; it's to speak naturally and confidently. If you speak too fast, how about measuring your rehearsals and trying to be just 5-10% slower each time? Or if you're too quiet, practice just one important part of your talk a bit more than you think you need to so you can nail that part of the final presentation.

Congratulations on making it through the steps in this chapter. Taking a hard look at your performance style is very challenging, but it's one of the most important steps to becoming a better version of yourself.

CHAPTER 8

Prepare: manage the details with care

In the days and hours before the presentation, there are a few final considerations that can make the difference between a good and a great presentation. A few are showstoppers: while unlikely, disasters are worth insuring against beforehand.

Polish the presentation: minimise distraction

The founders of one silicon valley startup are infamous amongst their colleagues for interrupting presentations and asking the presenter to fix a minor alignment problem or typo on a slide. It's an extreme example of a stakeholder wasting everyone's time (perhaps to signal to staff to make sure they sweat the details). The small mistakes really don't matter in the grand scheme of things; a minor alignment issue likely does not affect whether you've solved the real problems for users. But problems like this impact your credibility a tiny bit, and when they add up, they detract from the story you are telling.

You want to have the right conversation with stakeholders, so don't distract them with small details they might worry will affect users later. You're wasting their time and attention if you don't polish the work. In the worst cases, your stakeholders might judge your credibility or professionalism, assuming perhaps that you're lazy or not detail oriented. When glaring errors are staring people in the face, they can't *unsee* them. So how should we deal with the little corrections? Should we fix them as we're creating the work or later? The answer is both.

While you work

Small issues in design, like spelling, layout, kerning, and so on, should be dealt with in the moment, as much as is practical, without ruining your flow. If you're always ignoring spelling, you won't improve your spelling. It's a vicious cycle (unless there's some other reason you struggle, like dyslexia). You can also spot errors using modern tools, which can radically speed up the act of polishing the work. For example, you can use the snap guides in your design tools to make sure you've aligned things properly or tools that improve your grammar as you're writing.

Proof-reading

You will always overlook errors in the throes of creation. Therefore, it's critical to spend dedicated time reviewing your work, especially for a high-stakes presentation. A common trick for weeding out things you haven't noticed before is to shift your perspective a little bit. Before renowned film director James Cameron edits a movie, he flips all the film footage mirror-image style, so he can see the scenes he's been working on for months with fresh eyes. You could try printing out your slides or written speech and reviewing it that way instead of digitally. Or you could try taking a break from the work and returning to it a few days later. That fresh perspective can help you achieve quality when you've been staring at the work for too long.

TASK » Proof-read your presentation slowly, looking for mistakes in the content and the design.

The room: set it up for the best audience experience

It's easy to overlook the importance of the setting in which you will present. But a single detail can *completely* kill your presentation if you don't consider it beforehand. This is why theatre shows do technical rehearsals. Here are a few things to make sure you get right when setting up the room. At the back of this book, you'll find a handy checklist.

Screen size: Put your presentation on screen in the room (preferably with a slide showing some design work), then sit at the back and see if people can see the work clearly.

Lighting: An oft-overlooked element is how the lighting will affect what's on screen. You need to check the artificial light and the natural light and figure out what works best in the room. A useful default is to make the room darker, whichever way you can control it, as this will make the screen stand out.

Don't overlook the need to be visible yourself. This can be hard to do in a room you've made deliberately dark. Since the screen is probably more important on balance, don't worry if you can't get both right.

Cabling and control: It's gotten a little bit easier to use conference facilities with most laptops, but it's still a gamble if you're not familiar with the room. Make sure things work beforehand. Can you use the screen without an issue? Where will you place the laptop if you need to see the presenter screen? I've had to hack this repeatedly in poorly set up rooms, swapping out faulty HDMI cables, using my own longer ones, or borrowing adapters last minute. Professional presenters generally carry an assortment of cables and adapters with them to prepare for this very scenario.

Sound: If your presentation has sound, you need to make sure you can amplify it before showtime. That might mean using a dedicated speaker setup that you can plug into or routing the sound into the screen setup. Occasionally in a small setting, your laptop sound will be enough, but again, you need to test that beforehand. Professional presenters will sometimes travel with a small Bluetooth speaker for situations where the room needs it.

Microphone: In a larger conference-room space, you will occasionally find a microphone setup. It's worth at least trying it, even if you don't think you'll need it. You are the host; you're in control of the room. Amplifying your voice helps hold your audience's attention.

Test the volume with your speaking voice beforehand and adjust if necessary. Get used to holding the mic a few inches below your mouth; they weren't designed to be too close. You also need to adjust the volume to prevent feedback. When you do this, make sure you're standing in the place where you will present, as feedback depends also on where the microphone is pointing.

Seating and positioning: Here you must think like an event designer. How can you arrange the space to facilitate a good experience for the audience? How can you create a collaborative atmosphere?

You can try to dictate where people sit, but in my experience, senior stakeholders generally sit where they want to and don't like being told otherwise. That doesn't mean you can't arrange the seating to promote a better experience. For starters, check you have enough seats for all attendees and arrange seating to ensure that everyone can see the screen.

Where possible, you can facilitate more cooperative conversation by arranging chairs in a circle or oval. If it's a larger audience (over 8 people) and you need to moderate the Q+A, you might have to choose a more traditional audience arrangement with rows facing toward the front of the room. Making sure everyone has a line of sight is more important than how they will be arranged for discussion.

As you learned from my earlier story about the beanbag chairs, you also need to pay attention to the *type* of seating. Try to select chairs in the Goldilocks Zone of comfort—not so comfortable that people relax too much (like couches and beanbags) but also not actively uncomfortable (like metal folding chairs or school chairs).

In the past, I've resorted to swapping chairs from adjacent rooms when I felt that the seating wasn't right. Again, this seems like overkill, but it's one more detail that can affect how people receive your presentation.

Drinks and snacks: Although it is sometimes perceived as bribery, having drinks and snacks on hand is useful, not as a persuasion method, but to make the meeting feel inviting and relaxed. It also helps people stay engaged and energised. A good host looks after their guests.

Remote presentations: set up like a broadcaster

We often find remote meetings exhausting and socially awkward for good reason: human beings did not evolve to have conversations this way. We lose the nuances of body language, the easy informality of being together, the chit-chat at the beginning or end of the presentation, and most importantly, your ability to read the room.

Presenting to a remote audience is more like broadcasting; you are communicating information to an audience somewhere 'out there', with some two-way communication added in.

Put in some extra effort to make a remote meeting work well: working from home can leave us a little complacent about what we're wearing and what our room looks like.

Preparation

Where possible, use a videoconferencing tool that your stakeholders have already installed. The last thing you want is to be waiting for stakeholders to figure out how to use unfamiliar software in the first few minutes of your presentation.

Reading the room

You won't be able to read people like you can in physical space, but it's better to have some view than none. When presenting from a laptop, there's not enough real-estate to have the presentation, notes, and a view of the audience on screen. So whether you use a second screen, or a second device logged into the meeting (even your phone will do), find a way to see people on screen, and ask them to keep their cameras on.

Arranging your screen

Put some effort into designing the screen arrangement of your presentation windows. Here's a suggested priority order for the apps you might need on screen while presenting.

1. Presenter notes

2. Slides

3. Audience view

4. Chat window

Presenter notes come first because you must reference them throughout. Maintain more eye contact by positioning them near the camera. You want to balance how much attention you give your slides with the attention you give the audience.

Your appearance

You probably don't need to craft your on-camera appearance as much as, say, professional YouTubers do (unless it's *really* high-stakes), but it's worth spending more effort getting ready for a presentation than you normally would for a day-to-day virtual meeting.

Keep the focus on you by minimising distractions. Make yourself look tidy and presentable with clothing and makeup, but not so much that people would notice. Choose a neutral background, either in your room or by using a filter in your video-conferencing software.

Position your camera so you and at least some of your body are visible so you can use body language while you present. Position the camera level, centred, and close to the top of the screen you'll be looking at. Avoid looking down on your audience; This position doesn't encourage a feeling of connection. Besides, no one wants to look up your nose.

Make sure your face is reasonably well lit but be aware that adjusting the background light can be equally important. Software today is getting better at adjusting for large contrasts between background and foreground but test it to be sure.

Sound

The type of microphone you use for a virtual meeting has a subtle effect on the authority you project as the presenter. As deep voices carry more authority with people, it's in your interest to make sure you are not only heard, but that people can hear the full range of your voice. Professional microphones capture a wider spectrum of sound, particularly the bass range, than laptop ones do. A headset, clip-on, or standing mic will do a much better job of picking up your voice (even if they're cheap) than your laptop can.

Make sure doors are closed and that you select a place in your home or office where background noise is minimised.

Disasters: plan contingencies for worst-case scenarios

Murphy's Law holds that everything that can go wrong will eventually go wrong. Do enough presentations, and you'll get caught out. Create a little insurance for yourself in advance. When things go horribly wrong, the most important thing is to stay calm and flexible. If your laptop suddenly dies right before you're about to start the meeting, don't be the deer in the headlights. Panicking helps no one. A few simple acts of preparation mean you will have other options available to you and will reduce your likelihood of panic.

Most importantly, prepare backup presentation files and hardware. Whether it's access to a cloud copy on your phone or a PDF copy on a USB stick, make sure you've got backup access to the presentation file. Consider your points of hardware failure: a dead laptop or battery, missing cables, etc. Dedicate a few minutes of time before your presentation to figure out how easily you could switch to another laptop or device if needed.

Don't go it alone: designate a moderator, note-taker, and timekeeper

In his book, *Meeting Design*, Kevin Hoffman recommends that you assign several roles during meetings (based on the work of Doyle and Strauss).[13] You *can* do it all alone, but there's often too much going on for one person to handle effectively. Assign these roles to some willing colleagues in your team.

Discussion moderator

Since you're running the meeting, you will facilitate most of it. But when it's time for questions and answers, it's helpful to have someone else moderate the discussion so you can focus on answering questions about the design.

The moderator's job is to tell people how the discussion will take place, decide who will speak and for how long, and then make sure the discussion stays on topic. If possible, choose someone more senior than you to do this because they have more authority to interrupt people when needed.

NOTE » If the designs are the work of multiple designers, it's helpful to have three assigned roles: have one designer to present, another designer respond to questions, and someone else (designer or not) moderate.

Notetaker

Meetings need minutes or notes, especially when feedback needs to be addressed afterwards. Have one colleague capture the issues that come up during the Q&A. The more directly they can do this, the better. For example, consider leaving notes directly in your shared design tool for easy reference. Ask the notetaker to assign initials or names to any notes so you can track comments back to the people who gave them. This person should be skilled at identifying and summarising key discussion points; it's not their job to capture everything that is said word for word. It's also the notetaker's job to capture action items and summarise them at the end of the meeting.

Timekeeper

As you've carefully planned the presentation structure and timing (and rehearsed it to verify the length), it's helpful to have someone in the room whose only role is to monitor time. This helps you as much as stakeholders.

The timekeeper needs to let the room know when the following occurs:

Sections overrun: they can say something along these lines to interrupt politely so the conversation doesn't veer off track:

> **SAY »** (raises hand) "Hey, everyone. Just to let you know we're a little behind schedule. Let's find a way to get through the agenda."

Discussions overrun: Here, the timekeeper should emphasise the importance of the discussion while deferring it to ensure everyone sticks to the agenda.

> **SAY »** (raises hand) "I'm so sorry to interrupt the discussion. This is useful input for our team, but would it be OK for you two to return to this topic after the meeting and move on for now? I just want to ensure we get through the agenda and that everyone gets time to input."

CHAPTER 9

Discussion: translate unclear feedback into useful critique

> Convincing people is a social process. It's not based on intellect or superior arguments, and if you start there, it is likely to backfire. No one likes to be told they are wrong. Instead, you must first learn about the goals and problems other people have and find ways for your ideas to be useful on their terms.[14]

—Scott Berkun

No matter how carefully you've framed how healthy discussion should work, when it takes place, you will have to deal with difficult questions and feedback. Your principal task is *translation*. Stakeholders rarely know how to give thoughtful design critique, so you must transform what they're saying into something useful. Here's some extreme examples from a real project, courtesy of Jason Mesut:[15]

Stakeholder says...	What they meant...
I hate it	Not familiar to me, or where I had hoped to be taking this.
The bento boxes look terrible	It feels cluttered. I was hoping for something more clean and Swiss, in line with our brand.
It's shit	In banking, people are used to darker interfaces. My previous macho slick black platform was successful.
Get out	I'm angry that you've spent so much time doing this without engaging with me and being so far off the mark.

This is an enormous topic, worthy of a book in itself. If you want more in-depth guidance, read *Discussing Design* by Adam Connor and Aaron Irizarry. To start, here are six easy-to-remember responses you can use when responding to feedback in the moment.

The 6Ds of design discussion

	When to use it	What to do
1: Deference	As a first response...	listen and reflect back
2: Detail	If you can answer easily...	give your design rationale
3: Determine	If it's not clear what they mean...	translate by asking questions
4: Delay	If you can't answer now...	agree to follow-up
5: Document	If it's not clear, or you can't agree...	move the discussion to documents
6: Delegate	If it's not a design question...	refer to third party

NOTE » Real-life conversations are never easily reduced to a list of standard responses or a flowchart. Use these as a rough guide and combine or improvise with them. They're intended as a loose framework, not as fixed rules.

1: Deference

As a first response, listen and reflect back.

No matter what your initial reaction to a comment is, take it seriously. Acknowledge the stakeholder's input by reflecting back your understanding of what they've said. People respond well when you listen to and acknowledge them. And, as your collaborators, they might give you something useful, even if it's not obvious at first.

> **STAKEHOLDER:** "On the forms, don't we need to put the 'Next' button on the lower right-hand side instead of on the left?"
>
> **YOU:** "Okay, so your suggestion is that we move this button here? (Points at design). Tell me more about that."

Now you've shown that you're really listening to them before telling them what you think, even when they're solutionizing (which you asked them not to do). Start with this, and you'll have a much more productive conversation. Some example phrases:

- "So what I think you're saying is..."

- "If I've understood that correctly, you mean that..."

- "That's a good question to clarify..."

If a comment is particularly difficult to hear, it's sensible to pause for a moment. This will help you contain your initial reaction so you can give a more considered response. Remember that nothing they say is personal; it's about the design. You are not your design work. Use the advice in chapter ten to keep yourself grounded when facing difficult-to-hear feedback.

2: Detail

If you can answer easily, give your design rationale.

You might be able to give a simple, quick, satisfying answer right off the top of your head. In *Undercover User Experience Design,* Cennydd Bowles and James Box suggest that there's a hierarchy behind design rationale (adapted here), and you can use different types to strengthen the point you're making.[16]

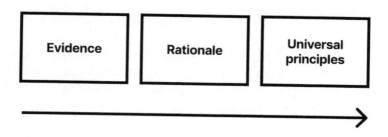

Let's look at three types of responses to this comment, starting with the strongest.

Evidence: Usually, evidence provides the strongest argument to support your rationale. Here's an example that combines qualitative and quantitative evidence:

YOU: "Yes, those are important. Even though your suggestions aren't shown in this top-level navigation, we have a good degree of confidence that people will be able to find them based on our research and testing.

We used two methods to work out the most user-friendly navigation. We generated ideas for the navigation using card-sorting. We put all the pages onto cards and had users group them according to what they thought were related concepts.

Once we understood how people organised the pages conceptually, we designed this navigation and tested it using a stripped-down version of the site—with just navigation. Through this tree-testing we know that 'Offers' is easily found under 'Shop.'"

Rationale: Sometimes, your rationale—the logic behind your design decisions—is all that's needed.

> **YOU:** "Those are good suggestions. In general, we try to keep navigation minimal just to make the browsing process fast. I'm cautious about adding anything to it. I think it's about understanding the context of use: when and why someone is using the navigation.
>
> For example, 'Buy' makes a lot of sense if you're selling a single product, but as we are selling many different products, then it makes more sense for people to click 'Products' in the nav, choose what they want, and then click 'Buy' on the page."

Universal principles: Many design decisions follow universal principles, but stakeholders often aren't aware of them.

> **YOU:** "Those are important options to present to a user. We've made this minimal because of choice paralysis. In short, the more options you give people, the harder it is to make a choice, a rule known as Hick's Law. That's why, in general, primary navigation tends to be 6 or 7 items at maximum. If we add more, we may slow users down."

You can use evidence, rationale, and universal principles in combination to be persuasive, but generally, you won't have all three available for every answer. You must figure out in the moment how to respond.

3: Determine

If it's not clear what they mean, translate by asking questions.

People sometimes ask questions that don't, at first, seem clear or constructive. Your job in this situation is to determine what they're *really* saying. Remember this is not their fault; it's difficult to articulate complex thoughts about design, especially when you're not a designer.

STAKEHOLDER: "I just don't think this screen is right. I'll know it when I see it, though. How about you keep trying and come back to us?"

Your strategy here is to give them the benefit of the doubt. Assume they have some useful feedback but are struggling to communicate it. Determine works as follows:

 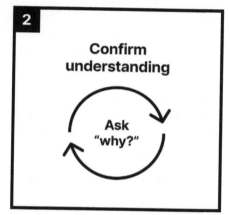

Step 1: Narrow the scope

The comment above is so vague, we need to create a boundary around what's relevant to better understand the issue this stakeholder has with your design. We can narrow the conversation by borrowing the critique framework from *Discussing Design*.[17] Summarise the objective of the design, whichever elements relate to that objective, and ask whether those elements are effective in achieving it.

Critique framework	You say...
What is the objective of the design?	Just to recap: the purpose of this screen is to help a user choose a tasty dish to order.
What elements of the design are related to the objective?	This list is there to entice them.
Are those elements effective in achieving the objective?	Is it stopping them from doing that?

Now you've narrowed the scope of the conversation, it's easier for both parties to resolve what's working, what's not, and why. Now they respond to this last question, you move to step 2, understanding why.

STAKEHOLDER: "Well, I think so. There's something... *off* about it."

Step 2: Confirm understanding, and ask why

From this point in the conversation, we will use two powerful strategies to translate what this person really means.

YOU: "Your concern is that there's something not working here. Why do you think that's the case?"

STAKEHOLDER: "I don't know. There's nothing wrong with the list items. I just feel like its purpose isn't clear."

YOU: "Oh, OK, so maybe there's something about the concept of it, or what it suggests it's for?"

STAKEHOLDER: "Yeah. Like the title of the list is 'Why not try.' I'm not really feeling that."

YOU: "Right. So in your opinion, there's something about that title that doesn't communicate why we're showing the list? What's going on there, do you think?"

STAKEHOLDER: "Yeah. I think if you could frame it in a better way, someone would understand that the items on this list are things we're recommending based on their taste."

What started with a vague, unhelpful comment is now a useful piece of feedback about the design. You've helped them to express a problem they could not articulate on their own. Translating comments like this won't always result in useful feedback or things to act on, but it results in much greater shared understanding.

TIP » If you can, avoid using the word 'Why' too directly at the start of sentences as it can seem confrontational.

Further tips

Find their agenda
Some comments have a not-so-obvious objective behind them. If you suspect this, you can ask questions to clarify what they might be fishing for. Start open-ended, e.g. "Which of the objectives do you feel is most impacted here?" and move toward the specific: "Are you concerned about the impact this will have on how many users sign up for the mailing list?"

Make taste feedback explicit
If a comment is a matter of taste, that's fine, but make it explicit: "Just so we're clear: your aesthetic preference is for the red?" By calling out that it's a matter of taste, it's easier to deal with. You can then explain your rationale and why that might be a better choice.

NOTE » *Determine* is the most difficult response suggested in this chapter; it's also the most useful. You can practise Step 2 (confirm understanding and ask why) in any conversation, not just in design. Try gently investigating a statement someone has made using questions while avoiding giving your opinion; it's a form of the Socratic method.

If you are still stuck trying to translate their point, then move to...

4: Delay

If you can't answer now, agree to follow up.

You don't have to be able to always answer all questions. You are not a performing monkey with a magic memory. If you don't have the answer right away, Delay.

Needs further consideration

STAKEHOLDER: "Have you tried blue for the headings?"

Imagine for a moment you find this suggestion unhelpful because you already know blue wouldn't work with the rest of the colour palette. But *they* don't know that. This is a hard thing to debate without them seeing it, so after some unproductive discussion, you say:

YOU: "OK, this could be a useful suggestion, but can I take some time to think about how it might affect the design, try it, and get back to you?"

Again, this might *seem* like a cop-out when you read it here, but you'll generally find that people respond well to someone being thoughtful about their idea. It will be much easier to deal with their suggestions when they're not around other people. Afterwards, you can show them that it's not a good idea without embarrassing them.

You can't remember the answer

STAKEHOLDER: "Why is that promo box below the heading instead of above? Surely, we need to remind them first?"

YOU: "Apologies. We designed that months ago now and off the top of my head, I can't remember the exact reason for that placement. Would it be OK for me to look at how the design evolved to remind myself why and get back to you with a considered response after this meeting?"

An alternative to this is to keep your iterations/alternatives handy at the end of your presentation; they're not your main narrative but can explain why changes were made or why something did or didn't work.

The discussion goes nowhere
You can also request a delay when you can't easily reach resolution.

YOU: "OK, I'm sensing that we could keep discussing this one element of the design for the rest of the meeting, and I'd like to make sure we have time for other questions. Would it be OK if we continue this discussion in documents?" (See below)

5: Document

If it's not clear, or you can't agree, move the discussion to documents.

Asking people to document what they think after the meeting is a good strategy because 'writing is thinking'. It forces someone to be clearer with their feedback.

Use it as a backup for Determine and Delay when:

• you can't agree, and you need to move on.

• their feedback isn't clear, and you can't tease it out of them in discussion.

When you suggest a follow-up discussion in documents, make it easy for the stakeholders to join in. Start the discussion on whatever tool or document you're using, and direct people to the right place.

6: Delegate

If someone asks about something other than design, refer it to the relevant party.

People may ask questions that fall outside of your responsibility. Listen out for them and delegate to brand, engineering, product, or whoever else is responsible.

> **STAKEHOLDER:** "Can't we have an export feature here too?"
>
> **YOU:** "Ah, yes, good suggestion. I think we are deferring that feature until later on our roadmap, but perhaps Dominique, our project manager, could answer this question?"

The key here is to avoid passing the buck. If, in the moment, you feel like avoiding responsibility for answering a difficult question, then don't delegate, *own it*. Delegation is only productive if the third party would have no issue with you referring a question to them.

Discuss outcomes: focus on the 'why' of the work

Much of what determines a good design discussion is how focussed it is on the outcomes. That's why you begin the presentation with objectives.

You've laid out in clear terms what your design work is trying to achieve for users and for the organisation. Imagine your meeting as a telescope aimed at the moon: these are the desired outcomes. When others bring in their own ideas and agendas, the telescope drifts away from the moon or loses focus. Your job is to keep the discussion coming back to the objectives, re-aiming to 'shoot for the moon'. When you feel the discussion is drifting, bring the focus back to outcomes, but be positive and curious about whatever someone is suggesting. Here's an example.

> **STAKEHOLDER:** "Have you thought about how to improve conversions on the sign-up page?"
>
> **YOU:** "That could be useful. To be honest, it's not high on our list of

things right now since the current objective is to improve how users choose food. We know how important that is, though; perhaps we can make it a focus of the next sprint?"

Inclusive discussion: get the most from everyone's input

Google's Project Aristotle attempted to find out the secret ingredient of the most effective teams.[18] They combed decades of data and studies, but no easy answers emerged. Eventually, they found some counterintuitive qualities effective teams tend to share.

One was equality in turn-taking. Teams that work well together are good at balanced conversations: when no individual dominates the conversation, everyone gets heard, and performance improves. As a facilitator, it's your job to make this happen. All too often, a senior stakeholder, feeling confident about their own opinion, will suck the air out of the room by blathering on and on, leaving no one else any time to give their input. While they might offer useful feedback, you want as many perspectives as possible and encourage anyone to speak up. Here are a few strategies to make your design discussions more inclusive.

Give people time to think and write first
One reason people don't speak out is that they haven't had time to gather their thoughts. One way to address this is with the reflection time we planned before discussion.

Work in the round
The simplest way to make sure you hear everyone's feedback is to order the discussion to cover everyone. With this strategy, you must be careful about monitoring time because everyone will have the expectation of being heard.

Prioritise the less powerful
It's common for well-represented groups (like white male leadership) to feel they can speak freely, while others feel there's no room for their input. If you start any discussion with people who are junior or under-represented, then you've signalled to everyone that their input counts.

Time-box each discussion

If you have a timekeeper on your team, enlist them to manage time, and determine roughly how much time each person might expect given the agenda. Discussions almost never fit neatly into these time-boxes, but at least the timekeeper will have a rough idea of when you're running out of time.

Interrupt politely

There's never a perfect way to interrupt, but sometimes the conversation goes on so long you have to. The best tactic to manage this is to set expectations at the start. Tell people that the timekeeper is there to keep the meeting on track and that they have permission to intervene.

If you need to interrupt, start by asking permission: "Is it OK to interrupt?", apologising, and then explaining: "It feels like we're having a really important discussion here, but if we carry on, we might not get time to discuss the whole design. Can I just check that leaving this issue until afterwards and moving on is OK with everyone?"

"Let others score"[19]

In *Pitching Ideas,* designer Jeroen van Geel discusses the frustrating moments when someone explains your idea back to you as though it's their own. As your job is to make everyone feel heard, you rarely need to claim back ownership of ideas or 'win' every discussion. Let go of the need to score points, even if it feels unjust. It's often better to let a stakeholder feel like they've had their way, especially when there are no consequences.

After the meeting: follow up with your stakeholders

It's easy to forget to follow-up afterwards when it feels like the job of presenting is done and dusted. But you should because people need the time and space to consider the work outside of the meeting and give more feedback if needed.

Send an email after the meeting in which you:

1. Thank them for their time. No matter what kind of feedback you receive, be grateful.

2. Recap any major action items that resulted from the meeting.

3. Invite them to one-on-one meetings to follow up on any points delayed.

4. Include a copy of or link to the presentation and design.

5. Show them where further discussion should take place, like within a collaborative document.

TIP » As per the guidance in Chapter 6, include more detail about the design in your slide deck when sending shared documents.

Resilience: manage yourself and your feelings

Dealing with difficult feelings is a part of any performance. Comedians, athletes, actors, dancers—anyone who has 'eyes on them' experiences crippling feelings of self-doubt in their career. With preparation, practice, and experience, your nerves will remain, but they'll be less overwhelming. People who perform often say that if they *didn't* have any nerves, they'd take it as a sign that they've stopped caring about their performance. Feeling nervous is natural because you care about things going well. Great performance does not depend on whether you're anxious but rather on what you do with that anxiety.

Finding emotional resilience isn't a one-size-fits-all task. Your thoughts and feelings are unique to you. How you manage them will be unique as well.

Key things to remember:

- You've got this! By using this book, you're already better prepared than you were before.

- People are on your side. Your stakeholders want you to succeed.

- You will notice your mistakes more than anyone else will.

- Negative self-talk, not nervousness, is the real enemy...

- So reframe those thoughts to be positive.

- Keep practising. The methods outlined in this book work, but not overnight.

Prepare and practice: the best way to reduce anxiety

The act of preparation is a way to reduce any anxiety you may feel about how the presentation will go. It almost doesn't matter how you prepare. Anything you do beforehand to crystallise what and how you will present will reduce any performance anxiety you have.

During the research for this book, I spoke to designers who recalled having panic attacks in the middle of a meeting: they'd often been pushed into situations where they didn't have time to prepare. A colleague was sick so they needed to present on their behalf; a client requested to meet at the last minute; the agenda wasn't clear. Situations like this happen every now and again, and they will teach you hard lessons about yourself.

Feeling like you're in control—having autonomy, being prepared, and determining how things will go—these are the keys to avoiding anxiety. That's why it's so important to spend *more* time than you think you need getting prepared, especially when the stakes are high. The more time you spend preparing when you're new to presenting, the more in control you will feel and the less of a problem your feelings will be in the future.

Expect the unexpected: adapt when problems arise

You cannot, and should not, try to control a meeting *too* much. Problems will occasionally arise outside of your control. Confidence means rolling with the punches, adapting when things don't work out the way you imagined they would.

"BEN: BE ALEXA"

I learned to expect the unexpected the hard way a few years ago. I was giving a talk at a conference in Brussels about voice interfaces. Playing sound clips was critical to my talk, but in the minutes right before I was due onstage, the sound wasn't working. Earlier that day, I'd watched a previous speaker leave the stage due to nerves, and I was on the edge of giving up as well. Instead, I walked out on stage, apologised for the lack of sound, and then just acted out all the dialogue myself.

I got quite a few laughs that day. The audience got to watch me play both parts along with the video, hamming up the exaggerated voices of users and then pretending to be Amazon's Alexa. I turned a show-stopping problem into an advantage—but only because I let go of perfection and embraced the problem. Staying flexible meant that technical difficulties took nothing away from my ability to engage the audience.

So far, your preparation has been mostly practical: rehearsing, checking the tech setup, ensuring proper seating, etc. One more thing you can do to reduce anxiety is to imagine every possible negative scenario. If you write them down, you'll be less surprised if any of them occur. In the practice of stoic philosophy, this is called negative visualisation; it's a way to desensitise your reactions to life's challenges. Note that this isn't an exercise in pessimism; you think about what *could* happen, not what *will* happen.

TASK » Write down 'what if...' statements about what *might* happen—all the things you're afraid of—and then think ahead about what you would do in that situation.

Self-awareness: reframe your negative thoughts

Cognitive Behavioural Therapy (CBT) is one of the most successful methods for dealing with your mental health. It works by acknowledging the intimate link between your thoughts and feelings. It's a feedback loop: a negative thought leads to strong feelings, which leads to more negative thoughts (and on and on). As these thoughts are often a distorted version of reality, CBT experts recommend reframing them into something positive or neutral. The process goes like this:

- Identify negative thoughts and feelings. "I'm going to make a fool of myself! I'm anxious!"

- Examine how that thought has distorted reality. "I'm really well prepared. My anxiety is trying to protect me."

- Reframe that thought. "I'm anxious because I care about the talk going well. I'm going to deliver a strong presentation."

- Feel different. "My anxiety has turned into excitement!"

If you practise this a few times, it can work wonders for your mental health. As the Buddhists say, "That voice in your head isn't *you*." Our brains will produce self-talk in response to feelings that can cripple us or lead to self-fulfilling outcomes. Let's look at the different ways our thoughts get distorted.

Cognitive distortions

Child psychologist Dr. Tina Rae teaches children a mantra to help them manage their thoughts and feelings: "What I think is not necessarily true or fact." Adults can benefit from the same thinking.

SCENARIO: Martha has a presentation tomorrow. She's just a few months into this job, and she's feeling scared about the impression she might make if she messes up.

> **MARTHA THINKS:** "I haven't presented to leadership before! They only gave me a few days' notice, the design isn't done, and I'm not prepared enough. It's highly likely I will look like an idiot!"

Catastrophising: exaggerating what's happening

"I haven't presented to leadership before!" With reframing, Martha realises she is catastrophising with this thought. While she hasn't presented to leadership before, she has met them all and found them mostly easy to get on with. She can see ways in which the meeting might go well.

> **MARTHA REFRAMES:** "I'm friendly with the people I'm presenting to, they will be a supportive audience."

"They only gave me a few days' notice." Whilst that is true, Martha realises this is *more* notice than the last time she had to present in her old job, and she *does* have enough time to prepare.

> **MARTHA REFRAMES:** "I have more time to prepare than I did last time!"

All or nothing: thinking of things in black-and-white terms

"The design isn't done." Is design *ever* really 'done'? Products are always made with incremental progress. They exist in multiple states over time. There's nothing left to do but be stoic and explain to those in the room that parts of the design are unfinished.

| **MARTHA REFRAMES:** "I'm showing them where we've got to so far."

Fortune telling: predicting an unknown future

"It's highly likely I will look like an idiot!" This is very unlikely. Martha is a talented designer who is well-prepared.

| **MARTHA REFRAMES:** "Even if I make a mistake, it's going to be OK. These
| people are on my side".

You'll know reframing is working when you feel a little relief as the reframed thoughts change your feelings. You can't take away the nerves completely, but you can do something more productive with them.

Visualise: mentally rehearse the performance

> I did a bad ride in Stuttgart in 2003 because I reacted to the previous guy's ride and didn't concentrate on myself, so I went out too fast. We used visualisation when I had a negative thought or anxiety. I would visualise the starting gate and each segment of the race. By race day I'd gone through it over 100 times.[20]
>
> —Chris Hoy, Olympic cycling champion

Chris learned visualisation from Steve Peters, the now-legendary psychiatrist who has helped hundreds of athletes like him attain their biggest goals. Steve gets athletes to focus their minds on *doing*. In Chris's case, this includes how he will think and act during an actual race. It's a mental rehearsal that helps reduce the mental noise that comes with giving a performance. It stops you from worrying about how you might mess up or how someone is going to react, and, instead, brings the mind back to what's most important: what you're going to do to perform well.

In practice

Let's say that in the past, you've struggled to hold people's attention during a presentation. This time you're committed to doing something different.

Your job at the start of this next presentation is to act like the host of a good party. You will hold the space, set the tone, and make sure people know that you are the one to listen to.

Visualise what confidence looks like in reality. Go through a mental rehearsal in which you enter the room with a confident stride. Your head is up. You smile while you greet everyone and speak a little louder than you normally would. While you set up your laptop, you break the ice with some light, conversation-starting question you prepared beforehand... and so on. Visualise the details of how this presentation will play out a few times to prepare yourself to make that vision a reality—and feel confident doing it.

Ground yourself: use mindful breathing

There's a secret power that comes from paying attention to your breathing. When presenting, there are two key moments where this is useful: right before you present and while you're discussing and responding to feedback.

To practise, try slowing your breath for a few minutes. Concentrate on a place where you can feel each breath (for example, the throat or stomach), and then gently observe your thoughts. I use this meditation throughout the day and even in meetings (with no one noticing!). The app on my smartwatch reminds me when to meditate and guides my breathing.

Staying grounded with breathing will make you a more relaxed and confident speaker. You'll be able to think and speak more clearly, and you'll be less likely to respond emotionally to challenging feedback.

Final thoughts

When we start our careers, many of us designers don't consider how important presenting will be to our success. Most of us get into this field because we like the quiet, solitary tasks the best: the creativity, the moments of personal inspiration, hours spent in solitude perfecting some idea on screen. But as Mike Monteiro reminds us, "design is a job". Presenting is a part of that job that very few designers get to avoid if they want their ideas to reach the world.

If you're starting your journey to better presentation skills, I hope this book has helped you, even if only a little. Your skill as a presenter is a work in progress, like your design. The worst outcome isn't delivering a bad presentation; it's giving up trying to improve because it didn't go as you expected.

Many years ago, I was given the dream job of designing a touch-screen interface for reading theatre scripts. I was so passionate about the subject I went overboard with the design. I even spent some of my own money hiring other designers and developers to help me build what I thought was a revolutionary product. I worked extra hard on the final presentation, including creating a working prototype I handed the client on an iPad as a final touch.

A year later, after a lengthy waterfall production process, the client launched a version of the product I didn't even recognize. I was struck with disappointment. After I'd left the project, people who weren't very design-savvy slowly watered it down until my design was all but gone. For a long time, I agonised over what I could have done differently. What could I have said to make them realise my design was the best one? How could I have been more persuasive?

While processing this soul-crushing event, I found some solace in stoic philosophy. Two quotes from Marcus Aurelius came to mind: "Just that you do the right thing. The rest doesn't matter," and "You have power over your mind—not outside events. Realise this, and you will find strength."[21]

I needed that reminder: I *did* do the right thing. The design work and the presentation were some of my best work. I let the outcome hurt me because I was disappointed in something I could not control. No matter how well we design or communicate, products are a collective act; we don't own them. We must try our hardest to make things right—and then be prepared to let go when things go wrong.

The ultimate measure of your presentation success isn't how well the design worked or what other people think. It's whether you did the right thing by *your* standards and how you responded when things don't go your way. Get a little better at telling the story of your design every time and tell yourself a kind one when you face adversity.

Useful extras

A few things I wrote didn't fit neatly into the structure of this book, but may still be useful to you.

The task checklist

Early preparation

- ☐ Map your audience's concerns and expertise
- ☐ Find and book a suitable meeting time and location (or virtual space)
- ☐ Send an invite that manages expectations about the presentation

Structure

- ☐ Create your outline horizontally on sticky notes
- ☐ Introductions and welcome
- ☐ Why this meeting
- ☐ Attention-grabber
- ☐ Principles
- ☐ Research insights
- ☐ Warnings and caveats
- ☐ Frame the feedback
- ☐ Scenario
- ☐ Map the highlights and lowlights of the user journey
- ☐ Outcomes
- ☐ Discussion (and format)
- ☐ Closing

Writing

- ☐ Record and transcribe a first draft
- ☐ Edit: First pass (basic clean-up)
- ☐ Edit: Analyse with writing aids
- ☐ Edit: Second pass (refine)
- ☐ Headlines
- ☐ Edit terms for consistency

Slides

- ☐ Design slides
- ☐ Leave space for extra content when sending/reading the slides

Rehearsing

- ☐ Record a rehearsal for 5-10 mins
- ☐ Transcribe it
- ☐ Measure your WPM (words per minute)
- ☐ Self-assess speed, volume, rhythm, and expression
- ☐ Summarise improvement tips onto cards
- ☐ Rehearse a few more times
- ☐ Ask kind and constructive peers for feedback

Before the presentation

- ☐ Polish: check slides for spelling and design mistakes
- ☐ Order drinks and snacks
- ☐ Prepare backup presentation files and hardware
- ☐ Prepare document version for sending + reading
- ☐ Assign helper roles: moderator, note-taker, timekeeper
- ☐ Negative visualisation: write down all the things that could go wrong
- ☐ Identify negative feelings and reframe

On the day

- ☐ Check screen and lighting
- ☐ Check cables, control, and sound
- ☐ Arrange seating
- ☐ Remote presentations: arrange your screen
- ☐ Remote presentations: check camera, sound, light, and background
- ☐ Visualise: mentally rehearse the performance
- ☐ Mindful breathing exercises
- ☐ Review your improvement tips

After the presentation

- ☐ Add action points to task list
- ☐ Send thank-you email with document version or links
- ☐ Book any agreed follow-up meetings

Reduce communication debt: use recorded presentations and huddles

High-stakes presentations aren't always the best method for keeping stakeholders informed about the progress of work or getting their input. Here are two other methods that encourage more frequent, informal collaboration.

1. The recorded presentation

If you're struggling to get everyone you need in the same meeting at once, one strategy is to record a short presentation and share it with everyone so they can listen to it on their own time. Working asynchronously like this will let you keep people up to date more frequently without the need to bring everyone together at the same time. It also alleviates some of the pressure of a big, formal meeting because you can record as many times as you need to and control the environment. This method also has the advantage of allowing people to view the content whenever they want and at their own pace.

A big disadvantage, however, is that you have no way to guarantee they will watch it. To increase the chances they will tune in, try to make the videos short and snappy. Avoid droning on in detail at all costs. Take what you think the length should be and halve it. Leave more detail and depth for meetings or documents. Always make sure there's room for discussion after sending, be it a follow-up meeting or in collaborative documents.

2. The regular wall huddle

One other way to reduce surprises is to meet informally and regularly in a collaborative space (like around a wall of work in progress). In one organisation I worked in, we scheduled a couple of hours every week where stakeholders could circulate through a handful of teams and get short, frequent updates on all their projects. These discussions worked well because of their informality. The more regularly you meet with people, the more you come to trust one another, which creates a sense of safety and camaraderie. People aren't as afraid to ask silly questions or challenge things with people they trust. Frequent communication makes people feel like they're working *together*, rather than working *for*.

Culture-fit: tailor the presentation to suit the organisation

David Foster Wallace once told a story about an older goldfish meeting two younger ones and remarking: "Morning boys. How's the water?" One of them later responds: "What the hell is water?" Culture is the water we swim every day. It's always there, and it has a profound impact on our environment, but we don't think about it that much. You may not even be aware of what kind of culture you're living in, even though you feel its effects every day.

Knowing the culture you're dealing with will give you an advantage throughout your process, and you will collaborate and persuade much more effectively. An organisation's culture has a fundamental impact on how it operates and what it values. You can work out which kind of culture your organisation has using Cameron and Quinn's Competing Values Framework (introduced to me by designer Kim Goodwin):[22]

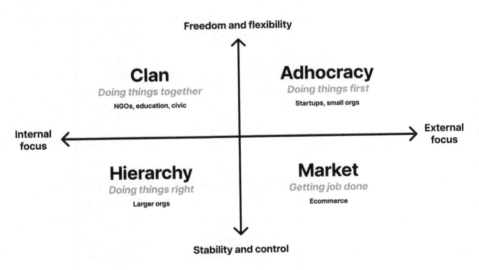

If you've identified which culture you're dealing with, use the tips below to consider how culture should affect the preparation and delivery of your presentation.

NOTE » Organisations don't always fall neatly into one category: they can be somewhere between two types across parts of the organisation or at different levels of seniority; modify your presentation accordingly. You must choose strategies depending on who you're presenting to.

Clans

These organisations love meetings. They're often non-commercial, like educational or governmental. They are highly inclusive, with an unspoken rule that everyone is included in decision-making. People don't feel safe to proceed unless everyone has been consulted. Your role in these organisations is like that of a coach or facilitator. Some tips for dealing with clans:

Be inclusive: Acknowledge the group by using 'we' over 'I'. This is a good idea in general, to make your work collaborative, but in clan culture, making people feel like part of a collective is critical. For example, when presenting any research insights, you could emphasise all the people you've consulted around the organisation.

Invite more people into the presentations than you think you need. Although larger groups make meetings less manageable, if you work in a clan culture, you are more likely to reach a consensus and progress quickly if you consult everyone before moving forward.

THE PLACEBO WORKSHOP

In a culture with a strong need for consensus, design can be a real challenge; these organisations make it easy for peripheral stakeholders to interfere. A university once hired me to redesign the website for hundreds of courses across dozens of departments. There wasn't time in the project to tailor the website to the needs of every department, but I knew that if I made them feel heard and did a good job presenting the design back to them, they were less likely to interfere later. I planned workshops for a large number of staff to gather input before the design work began. I knew full well that I might not get useful input on what users need, and if I did, I'd probably get too much of it. But my scheme worked. Later, there were almost no objections to the design. The stakeholders had just enough input to feel like they were heard.

Prepare for unexpected guests: People in clans will happily invite ten extra people to a meeting without letting you know. Your carefully prepared presentation can easily go off the rails in these situations. I once planned a two-hour workshop for six people, which turned into twenty-five without warning. They all wanted a say, and so I had to just roll with it — there was no way I could get through the whole agenda, so my workshop got cut in half. Being flexible in these situations is critical.

Hierarchies

These organisations thrive on process and certainty; they are control-driven. People within these organisations like to know exactly who approves something in the chain of command. Design thrives in ambiguity by avoiding solutions until problems are well understood, and hierarchical organisations are the least comfortable with this approach. Your role here is that of a process expert: you provide certainty and reduce risk by following an explicit process.

Emphasise predictability: Hierarchies love to know exactly how things work, so give them certainty. You can show a bit more of your process in these cultures to reassure stakeholders who are less familiar with design. Use things like Gantt charts and sign-off dates — do whatever you need to put more emphasis on when things are happening and why.

Clarify how sign-off works: Hierarchical organisations will often expect clear sign-off and approval procedures, and you need to know what they are, especially if they're complex or someone high up the chain of command (who is likely pressed for time) needs to review your work.

Know the chain of command: Leaders in hierarchical organisations are quite happy to ignore you if they deem you to be too junior. You have to know the right people to get your voice heard. If you don't already have direct access to senior leaders, make those close to them your allies—their direct reports, their assistants, etc. These people can open doors and translate key information for you.

Use the *nemawashi* method: This is an informal Japanese business practice, which loosely means 'meetings before meetings'. Decisions are made in pre-meeting meetings; presentations later to a wider group are just formalities. This can feel very inefficient, but it is a common and useful strategy to use in hierarchies. Because these cultures thrive on predictability and dislike surprises, you preview the work with leaders before a presentation. If, for example, there's a big decision to make, and you know that two senior leaders commonly disagree with each other, then you might go and take them through the work one-to-one beforehand. This process allows leaders to save face and avoid uncomfortable situations. If they disagree with something or feel they might ask a stupid question, they don't have to do it in front of everyone else.

Adhocracies

These cultures tend to exist in smaller, scrappier organisations, like start-ups. The rule of thumb is 'get shit done' any way you have to. It's more fun, free, and messy. These organisations don't like rules, strict processes, or a lot of formal bureaucracy. Your role is that of an improviser. You're someone comfortable with constantly changing plans, and you adapt yourself constantly to whatever arises.

Use impromptu meetings: In these organisations, you don't need to plan as much to get people's time. It's okay to just grab someone and update them quickly on a whiteboard. When a decision or input is needed, you can find the quickest way to do it.

Model some structure and process: Perversely, even though you can be looser with process in an adhocracy, it's in your interest to create just the right amount of structure. In an adhocracy, it's easy for decisions to get lost and undone with all the improvising that goes on. Be the person that brings a little rigour without seeming like you're spoiling everyone's fun: for example, following a process yourself, without being too explicit about it.

Be informal, not casual: In an adhocracy, people don't operate with consistency, for example, reliably using a meeting agenda or sharing meeting notes. As people are autonomous, they work in different ways around the organisation. This is risky because it can make you very casual about your work. Maybe you don't need to prepare for a presentation; you can just open your design tool and show something. But there's a difference between casual and informal. Being informal means you can have honest conversations about important work without worrying about politics or staying 'professional'; being casual means you're not prepared or thinking ahead. Make sure the work you're doing is deliberate. The laissez-faire nature of an adhocracy should not affect how seriously you take the quality of your work.

Markets

These cultures are the least common, but as the name suggests, they deal in numbers. People are reluctant to make decisions without numbers attached to them. It can make design challenging because the organisation doesn't handle qualitative decision-making well. They also like speed; dwelling on a decision is generally frowned upon. You take on the role of a data scientist, so...

Emphasise quantitative data: Without forgetting the importance of a good story about your users, include numerical evidence in your presentations (e.g. analytics), and refer to the key acronyms and metrics people care about. However, this is not about changing the way you make design decisions, it's about speaking the organisation's language.

Further reading

Many aspects of becoming a better presenter—storytelling, writing, discussing design, public speaking (and more) are so vast that whole books have been written about them. I hope I've armed you with enough information on each of these subjects to raise your presentation game, but if you want to learn more, I recommend checking out some of these great resources.

The Science of Storytelling by Will Storr
Strikes a great balance between the theory and history of storytelling—and what that means in practice.

Badass: Making Users Awesome by Kathy Sierra
Reframes how to think about products and what they're for. Shows you how to create products that make users the heroes of their own life story.

Design is a Job by Mike Monteiro
How to navigate the business of delivering design. Filled with wisdom about how to handle yourself, stakeholders, and clients.

On Writing Well by William Zinsser
Useful principles about writing non-fiction, suitable for many contexts, from emails to books. Read it to 'declutter' your writing. Helps you find a clear, strong voice in your writing.

Public Speaking Without Fear: How to Overcome Anxiety and Present with Confidence by Claire Cairns
Practical step-by-step guide to becoming a better, confident, and emotionally grounded version of yourself when performing.

Meeting Design by Kevin M. Hoffman
Most meetings aren't arranged with much deliberate intent. This book helps you design them to be productive and fun. (NOTE » the author is a contributor to this book).

Pitching Ideas by Jeroen van Geel

An invaluable, practical book for anyone selling an idea to an audience.

The Workshop Survival Guide by Rob Fitzpatrick and Devin Hunt

Not directly applicable to the business of presenting design but filled with useful advice about how to plan a great workshop. (Credit: Rob's other book, Write Useful Books, was used to create this book.)

Discussing Design: Improving Communication and Collaboration Through Critique by Adam Connor and Aaron Irrizary

Offers not just a great foundation for having conversations about design but aims towards the higher purpose of fostering a culture of constructive critique in your organisation.

Non-Violent Communication by Marshall Rosenberg

A method for dealing with yourself and others when conflict arises, and a life-changing philosophy for many readers.

Cognitive Behavioral Therapy: 7 Ways to Freedom from Anxiety, Depression, and Intrusive Thoughts by Lawrence Wallace

A highly practical approach to mental health that blends CBT, Buddhism, and stoic philosophy to help you reframe thoughts and feelings.

Final recommendation...

Join a local improv class. It's a nerve-racking experience, but there's no faster way to become comfortable with performance.

Notes

Introduction: Death by Screens

1. Mike Monteiro, *Design is a Job* (A Book Apart, 2012), 67.

2. Kathy Sierra, *Badass: Making Users Awesome* (O'Reilly, 2015), 51.

3. Stephen Johnson, "Kurt Vonnegut on the 8 'shapes' of stories," https://bigthink.com/high-culture/vonnegut-shapes/.

4. Jeff Gothelf, "The Power of Storytelling, TEDxYouth@ASBarcelona", 12 Sep 2022, https://www.youtube.com/watch?v=gsqMLmaLUCY.

Chapter 2. First steps: prepare early to save time later

5. Shai Danziger, Jonathan Levav, and Liora Avnaim-Pesso, "Extraneous factors in judicial decisions," PNAS (2011), https://doi.org/10.1073/pnas.1018033108.

Chapter 3. Structure part I: set the scene

6. Jared Spool, "The $300 Million Button", https://articles.uie.com/three_hund_million_button/.

Chapter 5. Sharpen your rationale with well-crafted words

7. Tanner Christensen, https://twitter.com/tannerc/status/1576635755794903040.

8. James Clear, https://twitter.com/jamesclear/status/1260998817450733570.

9. Darren Marranca, "10 Different Types of Headlines for When You're Stuck," https://fusecreate.com/10-different-types-of-headlines-for-when-youre-stuck/.

Chapter 7. Rehearsal: improve your performance with feedback

10. Chris Anderson, "How To Give a Killer Presentation", *Harvard Business Review,* June 2013, https://hbr.org/2013/06/how-to-give-a-killer-presentation.

11. Chunping Zheng, Lili Wang & Ching Sing Chai, "Self-assessment first or peer-assessment first: effects of video-based formative practice on learners' English public speaking anxiety and performance," Computer Assisted Language Learning (2021), https://doi.org/10.1080/09588221.2021.1946562.

12. Chris Voss, *Never Split the Difference: Negotiating as If Your Life Depended on It* (Random House, 2016).

Chapter 8. Prepare: manage the details with care

13. Kevin M. Hoffman, *Meeting Design* (Rosenfeld Media, 2018), 66.

Chapter 9. Discussion: translate unclear feedback into useful critique

14. Scott Berkun, "The Insiders Guide to Evangelizing Good Design", https://scottberkun.com/2021/the-insiders-guide-to-evangelizing-good-design/.

15. Jason Mesut, "Tactics for Amplifying the Strategic Value of Design", https://vimeo.com/228407872.

16. Cennydd Bowles and James Box, *Undercover User Experience Design* (New Riders, 2010).

17. Adam Connor and Aaron Irizarry, *Discussing Design*, (O'Reilly, 2015).

18. "Project Aristotle", https://rework.withgoogle.com/print/guides/5721312655835136/.

19. Jeroen van Geel, *Pitching Ideas*, (Bis Publishers, 2018), 143.

Chapter 10. Resilience: manage yourself and your feelings

20. William Fotheringham, "Meet the mechanic of the mind with an inside track on winning gold", *The Guardian*, May 2008, https://www.theguardian.com/sport/2008/may/08/4.

Final thoughts

21. Marcus Aurelis, *Meditations*

Useful extras

22. Kim S. Cameron, Robert E. Quinn, *Diagnosing and Changing Organizational Culture: Based on the Competing Values Framework* (Jossey Bass, 2011).

Acknowledgements

Dozens of people helped me create this book; it truly was a group effort over months and months. I'm grateful to all who gave me their time in putting it together: I couldn't have done it without your generosity! If I've missed anyone in these acknowledgements, I am truly sorry.

My wife, Sophia Passmore, has been an endless source of support and encouragement for my writing career. Without her wisdom and love, I may not have realised how much I wanted to write.

My parents have always provided me with the freedom to find my destiny. I'm grateful to them for the limitless support and stimulation in my childhood. They're smart people who never tried to mould me into a particular career.

I probably learned the most about performance from my drama teachers at Graveney School, Pete Maric and Kate Saunders. Both my career and this book would not have been possible without the supportive and generous design community around me, particularly Clearleft in Brighton, who gave me the opportunity to be a better designer, presenter, and writer.

The people who've helped in the production of this book are Rob Fitzpatrick for giving me a process to follow, James Gilyead for designing the book, Brooke Carey for editing my messy nonsense, Kyle Bean for the cover artwork, Kim Witten for the coaching, and James Box and James Bates for help with the creative concept and title.

The Write Useful Books community of authors encouraged me to keep going in our weekly writing accountability sessions. I would like to thank Marjorie Turner Hollman, Adam Rosen, Kate Warwick, Chris Davidson, Charli Prangley, Karin T. Wood, Brian Hall, and many others.

The people who've helped me with research and feedback on this book are numerous and, in some cases, anonymous! In no particular order, I'd like to thank: Adam Connor, Amy Nguyen, Sebastian Anupam Palma, Olly Boon, Konstantinos Spiliotopoulos, Mustafa Gokeri, Yemi Olaosebikan, Stuart De Ville, Selma Waley, Andreas Karamalikis, Ignacio Rovira, Oscar Morton, Kamila Mirash, Matt Hemmings, Carla Monfort, Paul Robert-Lloyd, Naomie

Curier-Araque, Matylda Kaczmarska, Danny van Burken, Andy Budd, Daniel Burka, Chris How, Alaistair Somerville, Scott Jenson, Dr Tina Rae, Dr Andrew Parkinson, Jeremy Keith, Matt Lindop, Giles Colborne, Patrick Potter, Carol Tang, Jason Mesut, Kate Zakrzewska, Julia Putnina, James Price, Shelton D'Souza, Oriol Valldeperas, Robert Wong, Jerlyn Marie Jareunpoon-Phillips, and many others.

Finally, the agency AndUs and their clients had a big part to play in making this book possible; I'd like to thank them for their flexibility and support.

Credits

Cover art by Kyle Bean – kylebean.co.uk

Cover design by James Gilyead – hustlersquad.net

Rashed Kemey https://unsplash.com/photos/oqYo9oVTa3k

Aleisha Kalina https://unsplash.com/photos/DQ_17uY9fjw

(photographer unknown) https://unsplash.com/photos/hNiNxhUfCfQ

About the author

Ben Sauer is a product and design leader, author and speaker.

As a UX Designer at the award-winning agency Clearleft, one of the first UX agencies in the world, Ben worked with clients such as the BBC, Penguin Random House, Tesco, and TCS to elevate their product design and user experience. His design for Evo magazine won Apple's Newsstand App of the Year, and redesigned the groundbreaking science journal eLife.

Ben later worked at Babylon Health, first as a Director of Design, and then Director of Product for AI. He led a large team of 100 designers, clinicians, data scientists, and engineers on AI-based products worth $100m+.

He's a seasoned writer and blogger, contributing writing to books like *The Great Redesign, Meeting Design*, and *Voice: The Speech Revolution*. He's spoken at numerous events and companies around the world: The Economist, The NEXT Conference, VW and Audi, UX London, Penguin Random House, UX Scotland, Reakt Breakpoint, Smart Voice Summit, and many others.

Ben has trained individuals and teams worldwide in design and product, particularly in conversational design, with his methods being adopted by teams at Amazon and the BBC. During his time teaching for O'Reilly, he taught people at NASA.

He offers training and workshops at bensauer.net for designers and teams looking to increase their strategic influence. He can be contacted at ben@bensauer.net

Enjoy this book?

Sign up for more presenting tips at:
deathbyscreens.co

Printed in Poland
by Amazon Fulfillment
Poland Sp. z o.o., Wrocław

21930633R00101